microwave cooking library™

microwaving america's favorites

microwave cooking library™

This cookbook is a collection of "tried and true" microwave recipes sent to us by readers and subscribers of the Microwave Cooking Library from all across America. We are pleased to share these family-tested favorites with you.

These recipes have been retested for use in all brands of microwave ovens by the Home Economists in the Cy DeCosse Incorporated Test Kitchens.

For best-tasting results, some recipes combine microwave cooking with conventional cooking, baking or broiling.

We know you and your family will enjoy *Microwaving America's Favorites.*

Staff Home Economists
Cy DeCosse Incorporated

CREDITS:
Design & Production: Cy DeCosse Incorporated
Senior Art Director: Bill Nelson
Art Director: Rebecca Gammelgaard
Managing Editor: Reneé Dignan
Editorial Assistant: Sally Stickel
Home Economists: Jill Crum, Peggy Lamb, Kathy Weber
Recipe Editor: Myrna Shaw
Production Consultant: Christine Watkins
Production Manager: Jim Bindas
Assistant Production Manager: Julie Churchill
Typesetting: Jennie Smith, Linda Schloegel, Bryan Trandem
Production Staff: Michelle Joy, Yelena Konrardy, Lisa Rosenthal,
  David Schelitzche, Cathleen Shannon, Nik Wogstad
Photographers: Tony Kubat, John Lauenstein, Mette Nielsen
Food Stylists: Teresa Rys, Susan Sinon, Suzanne Finley, Robin Krause,
  Lynn Lohmann, Susan Zechmann
Color Separations: La Cromolito
Printing: R.R. Donnelley & Sons (1186)

Additional volumes in the Microwave Cooking Library series are available from the publisher:

CY DE COSSE INCORPORATED
Chairman: Cy DeCosse
President: James B. Maus
Executive Vice President: William B. Jones

Library of Congress Cataloging-in-Publication Data.

Microwaving America's Favorites

(Microwave Cooking Library)
Includes index. 1. Cookery, American. 2. Microwave Cookery.
TX715.M634 1986   641.5   86-16607
ISBN 0-86573-518-2
ISBN 0-86573-519-0 (pbk.)

Published by Prentice Hall Press
A Division of Simon & Schuster, Inc., New York
ISBN 0-13-581893-1

Contents

Some of the best-tasting recipes in America are prepared by practical, creative cooks who know how to please their families' tastes every day of the year. These are the recipes that are passed among friends and neighbors, or "special" recipes that appear in the pages of church and club cookbooks. We are pleased to share these "tried and true" recipes in *Microwaving America's Favorites.*

These recipes come from all parts of the United States and Puerto Rico. Some are based on traditional ethnic foods

A. Elegant Stuffed Baked Potatoes
B. Hot Potato & Endive Salad
C. Pepper Steak
D. Raisin-Spice Loaf
E. Whole Grain Muffins
F. Triple Delicious Strawberry Pie
G. Betty's Pot Roast
H. Fresh Fruit-topped Cheesecake
I. Pork Roast & Gravy
J. Barbecued Chicken
K. Pickled Garden Relish
L. Cornbread Ring
M. Spiced Oriental-style Carrots
N. Marinated Pork Chops
O. Mexican Hot Dip
P. Shrimp Salad with Remoulade Sauce
Q. Chinese Orange Salad
R. Easy Beef Stew

handed down in families and adapted to microwave cooking. Others are original and combine microwave and conventional cooking methods. They range from a party-pleasing appetizer called "The Mountain" to a rich and delicious dessert called "Chocolate-Amaretto Cheesecake." Main dish entrees include delightfully light seafood ideas from the coastal areas to hearty beef recipes from the central plains.

Since microwave ovens vary in speed and size, each recipe has been tested and retested by our home economists to ensure successful results. We are certain you will discover new ideas to add to your menus when you start *Microwaving America's Favorites.*

Garlic Shrimp
Crab Meat Rounds
Hot Beef-Bacon & Cheese Dip

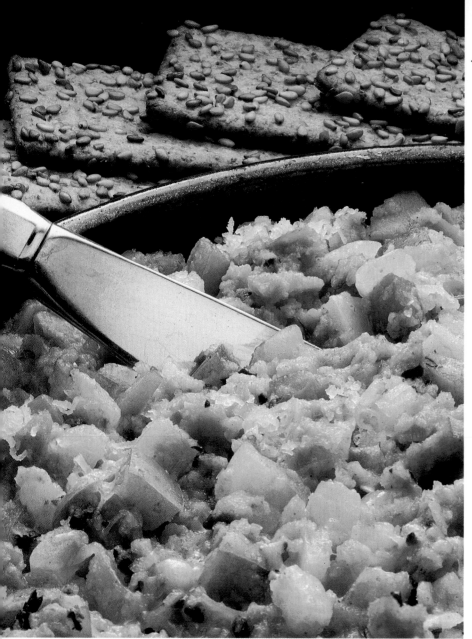

Gloria's Clam Topper ◀

Gloria Sanchez
Bethel, Connecticut

- 3 tablespoons butter or margarine
- 1 medium onion, chopped
- ½ medium green pepper, chopped
- 1 clove garlic, minced
- 1 teaspoon dried oregano leaves
- 1 teaspoon dried parsley flakes
- ⅛ to ¼ teaspoon dried crushed red pepper
- 2 cans (6½ oz. each) minced clams, drained (reserve 3 to 6 tablespoons liquid)
- 1 tablespoon lemon juice
- ½ cup seasoned dry bread crumbs
- 2 to 3 oz. Romano cheese, grated

1 cup

In 9-inch pie plate, combine butter, onion, green pepper, garlic, oregano, parsley and red pepper. Microwave at High for 4 to 6 minutes, or until onion and green pepper are tender, stirring once. Stir in clams, 3 tablespoons reserved liquid and lemon juice. Stir in bread crumbs. Add additional reserved liquid, 1 tablespoon at a time, until desired consistency. Sprinkle with grated cheese. Reduce power to 70% (Medium High). Microwave for 3 to 4 minutes, or until hot and cheese melts, rotating plate once or twice. Serve with crackers or Melba toast rounds.

Crab Meat Rounds

Sandra Rea
Baton Rouge, Louisiana

- 2 cans (6 oz. each) crab meat, rinsed, drained and cartilage removed
- ½ cup thinly sliced green onions
- ⅓ cup mayonnaise
- 2 tablespoons snipped fresh parsley
- ½ cup finely shredded Cheddar cheese
- 36 Melba toast rounds
  Paprika (optional)

3 dozen appetizers

In small mixing bowl, combine crab meat, onions, mayonnaise and parsley. Mix well. Stir in cheese. Set aside. Line 12-inch platter with 2 layers of paper towels. Spoon half of crab mixture onto 18 toast rounds. Arrange on prepared platter. Microwave at High for 1½ to 3 minutes, or until hot and cheese melts, rotating platter once or twice. Repeat with remaining ingredients. Garnish each appetizer with paprika.

Garlic Shrimp

Mrs. Pearl Lakey
Seymour, Missouri

It is very important to add oil in slow, thin stream for perfect mayonnaise.

Garlic Mayonnaise:
- 1¼ cups olive oil, divided
- 2 cloves garlic
- 1 egg
- 1 teaspoon dry mustard
- ½ teaspoon salt
- 3 tablespoons lemon juice

Shrimp Mixture:
- 3 tablespoons olive oil
- 2 teaspoons lemon juice
- 2 cloves garlic, each cut into 4 pieces
- 1 bay leaf
- ¼ teaspoon salt
- ¼ teaspoon dried thyme leaves
- ⅛ teaspoon pepper
- ½ lb. medium shrimp, shelled and deveined

4 servings.

In blender bowl, combine ¼ cup olive oil, garlic, egg, dry mustard and salt. Blend at medium high speed until well mixed. With blender running, slowly add ½ cup olive oil in very thin stream. Slowly add lemon juice, stopping to scrape sides, if needed. With blender running, add remaining ½ cup olive oil in very thin stream, stopping to scrape sides, if needed. Mixture should be smooth and thick. Chill several hours to blend flavors.

In 1-quart casserole, combine all Shrimp Mixture ingredients, except shrimp. Cover. Microwave at 70% (Medium High) for 3½ to 5½ minutes, or until garlic is light golden, stirring once. Remove garlic. Add shrimp. Stir to coat. Re-cover. Microwave at 70% (Medium High) for 2 to 4 minutes, or until shrimp are opaque, stirring once or twice. Let stand, covered, for 2 minutes. Remove bay leaf. Serve with Garlic Mayonnaise.

Hot Crab Fondue ▲

Sandra J. Robinson
Sicklerville, New Jersey

- 2 pkgs. (8 oz. each) cream cheese
- 2 jars (5 oz. each) sharp pasteurized process cheese spread
- ½ cup half-and-half
- 1 teaspoon Worcestershire sauce
- ⅛ teaspoon garlic powder
- ⅛ teaspoon cayenne
- 2 cans (6 oz. each) crab meat, rinsed, drained and cartilage removed

About 4 cups

In 2-quart casserole, combine all ingredients, except crab meat. Microwave at 70% (Medium High) for 3 to 6 minutes, or until mixture is smooth, stirring 2 or 3 times with whisk. Stir in crab meat. Microwave at 70% (Medium High) for 1 to 2 minutes, or until heated through. Serve with rye and pumpernickel bread cubes for dipping.

The Mountain

Janice L. Gritz
New York, New York

A combination of two favorite dips, piled high and full of color.

- 1 lb. lean ground beef
- 1 jar (8 oz.) hot salsa or jalapeño relish, divided
- ¼ teaspoon salt
- ¼ teaspoon onion powder
- ¼ teaspoon garlic powder
- ⅛ teaspoon pepper
- 1 can (16 oz.) refried beans
- 1½ cups shredded Cheddar cheese
- 1½ cups shredded Monterey Jack cheese
- Chopped tomatoes
- Sliced green onions
- Sliced black olives
- Dairy sour cream
- Guacamole
- Tortilla or corn chips

10 to 12 servings

How to Microwave The Mountain

Crumble beef into 2-quart casserole. Stir in ½ cup salsa, salt, onion powder, garlic powder and pepper. Cover.

Microwave at High for 4 to 6 minutes, or until beef is no longer pink, stirring once or twice to break apart. Drain.

Stir in remaining ½ cup salsa and beans. On 12-inch platter, mound mixture into rounded shape, about 9 inches.

Mix cheeses together. Sprinkle over meat and bean mixture, covering completely.

Microwave at 50% (Medium) for 7 to 10 minutes, or until cheese melts, rotating platter after every 2 minutes.

Sprinkle tomatoes, onions and olives in center of cheese. Alternate dollops of sour cream and guacamole around edge of platter. Serve with tortilla chips.

Swedish Meatballs ▲

Recipe was developed by Nancy and her father.

Nancy M. Heider
Larson, Wisconsin

Meatballs:
- ¼ cup finely chopped onion
- 1 tablespoon butter or margarine
- ½ lb. lean ground beef
- ¼ lb. ground pork
- ¼ lb. ground veal
- ⅓ cup unseasoned dry bread crumbs
- ¼ cup milk
- 1 egg, beaten
- ½ teaspoon ground cardamom
- ½ teaspoon ground allspice
- ½ teaspoon ground nutmeg
- ½ teaspoon salt
- ¼ teaspoon dried dill weed
- ⅛ teaspoon pepper

Gravy:
- 1 envelope (1.8 oz.) oxtail soup mix
- 1¼ cups cold water

About 4 dozen appetizers

In small bowl, combine onion and butter. Cover with plastic wrap. Microwave at High for 1 to 2 minutes, or until onion is tender. In medium mixing bowl, combine onion mixture and remaining meatball ingredients. Mix well. For fine-textured meatballs, mix ingredients in food processor. Shape into 48 meatballs, about ¾ inch each. Place in 10-inch square casserole. Set aside.

In 4-cup measure, blend soup mix and water with whisk. Microwave at High for 4 to 6 minutes, or until mixture thickens and bubbles, blending with whisk after every 2 minutes. Set aside. Cover meatballs with wax paper. Microwave at High for 5 to 9 minutes, or until meatballs are firm and cooked through, stirring once or twice. Drain. Pour gravy over meatballs. Stir to coat. Microwave at High for 30 seconds to 1 minute, or until hot.

Oodles o' Oysters

Mrs. Tally Orange
Paw Paw, Michigan

- 1 cup butter or margarine
- 1½ teaspoons celery salt
- ½ teaspoon onion powder
- ¼ teaspoon garlic powder
- 5 to 6 cups oyster crackers
- ½ cup grated Parmesan cheese

5 to 6 cups

Place butter in large mixing bowl. Microwave at High for 2 to 3 minutes, or until butter melts. Stir in celery salt, onion powder and garlic powder. Add crackers. Stir to coat. Mix in cheese. Pour onto baking sheet. Cool completely. Store in covered container.

Broccoli Dip ▲

A popular and versatile hot dip.

*Marge Clayton
Highland, Illinois*

1 pkg. (10 oz.) frozen chopped
  broccoli
1 small onion, chopped
1 can (10¾ oz.) condensed
  cream of mushroom soup
2 pkgs. (4 oz. each)
  Neufchâtel garlic cheese
  spread

1 jar (4½ oz.) sliced
  mushrooms, drained
1 pkg. (2¾ oz.) sliced almonds
1 teaspoon Worcestershire
  sauce
½ teaspoon salt
¼ teaspoon pepper
¼ teaspoon hot pepper sauce

4 cups

In 1½-quart casserole, combine broccoli and onion. Cover. Microwave at High for 5 to 6 minutes, or until broccoli is defrosted and onion is tender, stirring 2 or 3 times. Drain thoroughly. Stir in remaining ingredients. Re-cover. Reduce power to 70% (Medium High). Microwave for 5 to 6 minutes, or until mixture is heated through, stirring after every 2 minutes. Serve with assorted crackers.

Spinach Dip: Follow recipe above, substituting frozen chopped spinach for broccoli. Press defrosted spinach to remove excess moisture. Continue as directed.

Hot Beef-Bacon & Cheese Dip

*Teresa A. Bratton
Portsmouth, Ohio*

3 slices bacon
1 pkg. (3 oz.) cream cheese
1 pkg. (2½ oz.) smoked sliced
  beef, finely chopped
½ cup finely shredded
  Cheddar cheese
2 tablespoons milk
2 green onions, thinly sliced

1 cup

Arrange bacon on roasting rack. Cover with paper towel. Microwave at High for 2½ to 4 minutes, or until brown and crisp. Cool slightly. Crumble. Place bacon in small mixing bowl or serving dish. Stir in remaining ingredients, except onions. Microwave at 70% (Medium High) for 3 to 4 minutes, or until cheese melts, stirring once. Top with onions. Serve hot with assorted crackers.

◄ Mexican Hot Dip

Nancy J. Klein
Eugene, Oregon

1 lb. lean ground beef
1 medium green pepper,
   chopped
1 pkg. (1.4 oz.) taco
   seasoning mix
2 cups shredded Cheddar
   cheese

1 can (16 oz.) refried beans
1 can (8 oz.) tomato sauce
⅓ cup jalapeño relish
   Sliced green onions
   (optional)
   Dairy sour cream (optional)

About 5½ cups

Crumble beef into 2-quart casserole. Stir in green pepper and taco seasoning mix. Cover. Microwave at High for 5 to 6 minutes, or until beef is no longer pink, stirring once to break apart. Stir in cheese, beans, tomato sauce and jalapeño relish. Microwave, uncovered, at High for 5 to 9 minutes, or until hot and cheese melts, stirring twice. Garnish with green onions and sour cream. Serve hot with tortilla or corn chips.

◄ Chile con Queso

Ginger L. Johnson
Phoenixville, Pennsylvania

1 lb. pasteurized process
   cheese spread, cut into
   1-inch cubes
1 can (10¾ oz.) condensed
   cream of mushroom soup

1 can (4 oz.) chopped green
   chilies, drained
⅛ teaspoon garlic powder
   Sliced jalapeño pepper
   (optional)

About 3½ cups

In 1½-quart casserole, combine all ingredients, except jalapeño pepper. Mix well. Microwave at 70% (Medium High) for 8 to 10 minutes, or until mixture can be stirred smooth, stirring after every 2 minutes. Garnish with jalapeño pepper. Serve hot with tortilla or corn chips.

◄ Bean Dip

Beverley J. Clarke
Woodbridge, Connecticut

1 lb. lean ground beef
1 cup chopped onion,
   divided
1 tablespoon chili powder
1 can (16 oz.) spicy refried
   beans

½ cup catsup
¾ teaspoon salt
½ cup sliced black olives
½ cup shredded sharp
   Cheddar cheese

About 5 cups

Crumble beef into 9-inch round baking dish. Stir in ½ cup onion and chili powder. Microwave at High for 4½ to 6½ minutes, or until beef is no longer pink, stirring once to break apart. Stir in beans, catsup and salt. Reduce power to 50% (Medium). Microwave for 7 to 10 minutes, or until hot, stirring twice. Sprinkle with remaining ½ cup onion, olives and cheese. Microwave at High for 2 to 3 minutes, or until cheese melts, rotating dish once. Serve hot with corn chips.

Candied Spiced Nuts

Mary Agnes Whiting
Sharpsburg, Georgia

A smash hit at parties.

    1 cup pecan halves
    1 cup walnut halves
   ¾ cup dry roasted peanuts
   ¾ cup cashews
    1 cup sugar
   ½ cup water
    2 teaspoons pumpkin pie
       spice
   ½ teaspoon salt

                        3½ cups

How to Microwave Candied Spiced Nuts

Combine pecans, walnuts, peanuts and cashews in medium mixing bowl. Set aside. In 3-quart casserole, mix sugar, water, pumpkin pie spice and salt. Cover. Microwave at High for 3 minutes. Stir well.

Insert microwave candy thermometer. Microwave, uncovered, at High for 6 to 10 minutes, or until thermometer registers 234°F (soft ball stage). Syrup forms a soft ball which flattens when removed from cold water.

Stir in nuts until coated with sugar mixture. Spread on wax paper. Let stand until firm. Store in airtight container.

Caramel Corn

Sandra M. Waske
Canton, New York

 8 to 10 cups popped
      popcorn
1½ cups dry roasted peanuts
 1 cup packed brown sugar
 ½ cup butter or margarine
 ¼ cup light corn syrup
 ½ teaspoon salt
 ½ teaspoon baking soda
 ½ teaspoon vanilla, optional

About 10 cups

In 5-quart casserole, combine popcorn and peanuts. Mix well. Set aside. In 2-quart measure or casserole, combine brown sugar, butter, corn syrup and salt. Mix well. Microwave at High for 3 to 5 minutes, or until sugar is dissolved and mixture is boiling, stirring after every minute. Insert microwave candy thermometer. Microwave at High for 2 to 4½ minutes, or until thermometer registers 280°F (soft crack stage). Syrup separates into hard but not brittle threads when dropped into cold water. Stir in baking soda and vanilla. Pour hot mixture quickly over popcorn and peanuts, stirring to coat. Microwave at High for 3 minutes, stirring after half the time. Spread on wax paper-lined baking sheet. Cool. Break into small pieces.

Molasses Corn

Carol A. Bodenhorn
Monongahela, Pennsylvania

 4 to 5 cups popped popcorn
 ¾ cup peanuts
 ⅓ cup molasses
 ¼ cup packed brown sugar

 2 tablespoons butter or
      margarine
 ¼ teaspoon vinegar
 ⅛ teaspoon salt

About 6 cups

In 3-quart casserole, combine popcorn and peanuts. Mix well. Set aside. In 2-quart measure or casserole, combine molasses, brown sugar, butter, vinegar and salt. Mix well. Microwave at High for 1½ to 3 minutes, or until sugar is dissolved and mixture is boiling, stirring after every minute. Insert microwave candy thermometer. Microwave at High for 2½ to 3½ minutes, or until thermometer registers 280°F (soft crack stage). Syrup separates into hard but not brittle threads when dropped into cold water. Pour hot mixture quickly over popcorn and peanuts, stirring to coat. Microwave at High for 1½ minutes, stirring once. Spread on wax paper-lined baking sheet. Cool. Break into small pieces.

Soups

Confetti Soup

Cauliflower-Blue Cheese Soup

Clara C. Carli
North Arlington, New Jersey

- 1½ cups sliced zucchini, ¼ inch thick
- 1½ cups fresh cauliflowerets, 1-inch pieces
- ¼ cup water
- 2½ cups half-and-half, divided
- 3 tablespoons all-purpose flour
- 1 tablespoon instant chicken bouillon granules
- 2 egg yolks, beaten
- ⅓ cup crumbled blue cheese (2 oz.)

3 to 4 servings

In 2-quart casserole, combine zucchini, cauliflower and water. Cover. Microwave at High for 5 to 6 minutes, or until zucchini is tender-crisp, stirring once. Set aside. Place ½ cup half-and-half in 4-cup measure. Stir in flour and bouillon. Blend in remaining 2 cups half-and-half. Stir flour mixture into vegetables. Reduce power to 70% (Medium High). Microwave, uncovered, for 9 to 14 minutes, or until mixture thickens and bubbles, stirring after every 3 minutes.

Beat small amount of hot mixture into egg yolks. Return egg yolk mixture to soup, stirring constantly. Stir in blue cheese. Reduce power to 50% (Medium). Microwave for 2 minutes, or until heated through.

Country Potato-Cheese Soup

Susanne Adams
Livingston, Montana

- 2½ cups cubed potatoes, ¼-inch cubes
- 1 cup chopped carrots
- ½ cup chopped celery
- ½ cup chopped onion
- 1 cup hot water, divided
- 2 teaspoons instant chicken bouillon granules
- ½ teaspoon salt
- ⅛ teaspoon pepper
- 1 cup milk
- 1 cup shredded Cheddar cheese

4 to 6 servings

In 2-quart casserole, combine potatoes, carrots, celery, onion, ¼ cup water, bouillon, salt and pepper. Cover. Microwave at High for 10 to 13 minutes, or until vegetables are tender, stirring once. Pour into food processor or blender bowl. Process until coarsely puréed. Return vegetable mixture to casserole. Blend in remaining ¾ cup water and the milk. Stir in cheese. Re-cover. Microwave at High for 1½ to 3½ minutes, or until cheese melts, stirring once or twice.

Smoky Bean Soup

Sharon Allen
Wichita, Kansas

1 cup dried Great Northern
    beans, rinsed and sorted
1 cup dried pinto beans,
    rinsed and sorted
6 cups hot water
2 bay leaves
1 large onion, chopped
1 clove garlic, minced
1 teaspoon salt
½ teaspoon dried thyme leaves
½ teaspoon pepper
1 to 1½ teaspoons liquid
    smoke
¼ cup packed brown sugar,
    optional
1 ham hock
    or ham bone
1 can (8 oz.) tomato sauce

8 to 10 servings

In 5-quart casserole, combine Great Northern and pinto beans, water, bay leaves, onion, garlic, salt, thyme, pepper and liquid smoke. Cover. Microwave at High for 10 to 15 minutes, or until boiling. Let stand, covered, for 1 hour. Stir in brown sugar. Add ham hock. Re-cover. Microwave at High for 5 minutes. Reduce power to 50% (Medium). Microwave for 1 hour, turning ham hock over and stirring after every 20 minutes. Remove ham hock. Cut ham from bone. Return ham to soup. Discard bone. Stir in tomato sauce. Re-cover. Microwave at 50% (Medium) for 45 minutes to 1¼ hours, or until beans are tender, stirring once. Remove bay leaves.

Variation:

Follow recipe above, substituting 1½ to 2 cups cubed fully cooked ham for ham hock.

Cheesy Vegetable Soup ▲

Darlene A. Withrow
Marinette, Wisconsin

2 cups frozen broccoli,
    cauliflower and carrot
    mixture
1 cup peeled cubed potato,
    ¼-inch cubes
½ cup chopped onion
½ cup chopped celery

1 can (14½ oz.) ready-to-serve
    chicken broth
1 can (10¾ oz.) condensed
    cream of mushroom soup
½ lb. pasteurized process
    cheese spread, cut into
    ½-inch cubes

4 to 6 servings

In 2-quart casserole, combine frozen vegetable mixture, potato, onion and celery. Cover. Microwave at High for 7 to 10 minutes, or until vegetables are tender, stirring once. Mash vegetables slightly if desired. Mix in remaining ingredients. Re-cover. Microwave at High for 6 to 9 minutes, or until cheese melts and mixture can be stirred smooth, stirring twice.

21

◄ Strawberry Soup

Barb Gray
Ballwin, Missouri

Serve very cold as a first course soup.

- 1 quart ripe strawberries, washed and hulled
- 2 tablespoons lemon juice
- 1½ cups hot water
- ½ cup sugar
- 1 tablespoon quick-cooking tapioca
- ½ cup sweet white wine
  Dairy sour cream or yogurt (optional)

6 to 8 servings

In food processor or blender bowl, combine strawberries and lemon juice. Process until smooth. Pour into 2-quart casserole. Stir in hot water, sugar and tapioca. Cover. Microwave at 70% (Medium High) for 12 to 17 minutes, or until tapioca is translucent, stirring 2 or 3 times. Stir in wine. Chill for at least 4 hours. Garnish with dollop of sour cream, if desired.

Cream of Tomato Soup ▲

Jeanne L. Wingert
Mondovi, Wisconsin

- 2 tablespoons butter or margarine
- 1 tablespoon finely chopped onion
- 3 tablespoons all-purpose flour
- 1 teaspoon salt
- 1 teaspoon sugar
- ¼ teaspoon dried marjoram leaves
  Dash pepper
- 1 can (16 oz.) stewed tomatoes, puréed
- 2 cups milk

4 servings

In 1-quart casserole, combine butter and onion. Microwave at High for 2 minutes. Stir in flour, salt, sugar, marjoram and pepper. Blend in tomatoes. Microwave at High for 3 to 6 minutes, or until mixture thickens and bubbles, stirring twice. Set aside. Place milk in 2-cup measure. Microwave at High for 2 to 3 minutes, or until hot. Blend hot milk into tomato mixture, stirring with whisk. Microwave at High for 2 to 4 minutes, or until heated through.

Chilled Carrot Soup

Captain John F. Vandegrift, Sr.
Groves, Texas

- 1 cup chopped carrots
- 1 large potato, peeled and chopped
- 1 medium leek, white part only, chopped
- 1 can (14½ oz.) ready-to-serve chicken broth
- 1 tablespoon fresh lemon juice
- ¼ teaspoon salt
- ¼ teaspoon dried summer savory leaves
- ⅛ teaspoon ground nutmeg
- ⅛ teaspoon pepper
- 1 cup half-and-half

3 to 4 servings

In 1½-quart casserole, combine all ingredients, except half-and-half. Mix well. Cover. Microwave at High for 20 to 25 minutes, or until vegetables are very tender, stirring twice. Let stand, covered, for 5 minutes. Pour into blender or food processor bowl. Process until smooth. Return vegetable mixture to casserole. Blend in half-and-half. Re-cover. Chill for at least 4 hours.

Sherried Leek Soup

John R. Fuhrbach
Amarillo, Texas

¼ cup butter or margarine, cut up
3 to 4 medium leeks, cut in half lengthwise and thinly sliced
1 can (10¾ oz.) condensed chicken broth, divided
½ teaspoon salt
¼ to ½ teaspoon pepper
2 cups peeled cubed potatoes, ¼-inch cubes
1½ cups milk
½ cup whipping cream
¼ cup sherry

6 to 8 servings

In 2-quart casserole, combine butter, leeks, ¼ cup broth, salt and pepper. Cover. Microwave at High for 7 to 13 minutes, or until leeks are tender, stirring once. Set aside. In 1-quart casserole, combine potatoes and ¼ cup broth. Cover. Microwave at High for 6 to 8 minutes, or until potatoes are tender, stirring once.

Beat potatoes and remaining broth with electric mixer or in food processor bowl until smooth. Add to leek mixture. Blend in milk and cream. Re-cover. Reduce power to 70% (Medium High). Microwave for 7 to 10 minutes, or until heated through, stirring after every 3 minutes. Stir in sherry.

Lentil Soup

Edith H. Hancock
Lakewood, New Jersey

1 small onion, finely chopped
1 clove garlic, minced
1 tablespoon olive oil
1¼ cups dried lentils, rinsed and sorted
6 cups hot water
2 medium carrots, thinly sliced
1 large stalk celery, finely chopped

1 medium potato, cut into ½-inch cubes
1 can (8 oz.) tomato sauce
½ cup cubed fully cooked ham or pork, ¼-inch cubes
½ teaspoon dried marjoram leaves
Salt

6 to 8 servings

In 3-quart casserole, combine onion, garlic and olive oil. Cover. Microwave at High for 2 to 3 minutes, or until onion is tender. Stir in remaining ingredients, except salt. Re-cover. Microwave at High for 5 minutes. Reduce power to 70% (Medium High). Microwave for 45 minutes to 1 hour, or until lentils are tender, stirring 2 or 3 times. Stir in salt to taste.

Confetti Soup

Nancy Olson
Belgrade, Minnesota

- 3 tablespoons butter or margarine
- 1 cup cubed carrots, ¼-inch cubes
- 1 cup cubed rutabaga, ¼-inch cubes
- ½ cup chopped onion
- ½ cup chopped celery
- 1 cup fresh broccoli flowerets or cauliflowerets
- ¼ cup all-purpose flour
- ½ teaspoon salt
- ½ teaspoon pepper
- ¼ teaspoon sugar
- 4 cups milk
- 1 cup shredded pasteurized process American cheese
- 1 cup frozen corn
- ½ cup cubed fully cooked ham, ¼-inch cubes
- ½ cup frozen peas

5 to 6 servings

In 3-quart casserole, combine butter, carrots, rutabaga, onion, celery and broccoli. Cover. Microwave at High for 9 to 14 minutes, or until vegetables are tender, stirring 3 times. Stir in flour, salt, pepper and sugar. Blend in milk. Reduce power to 70% (Medium High). Microwave, uncovered, for 15 to 18 minutes, or until mixture is slightly thickened, stirring after every 4 minutes. Stir in cheese, corn, ham and peas. Microwave at 70% (Medium High) for 3 to 5 minutes, or until heated through and cheese melts, stirring once.

Puerto Rican Bean Soup ▲

Gail Rosario
Albuquerque, New Mexico

- 1½ cups uncooked broken spaghetti
- 1 lb. fully cooked Polish sausage, cut into ¼-inch cubes
- 1 medium onion, chopped
- ½ medium green pepper, chopped
- 1 tablespoon chili powder
- 1 teaspoon salt
- 1 teaspoon garlic powder
- ½ teaspoon dried basil leaves
- ½ teaspoon dried oregano leaves
- 2 cans (15 oz. each) kidney beans, drained
- 4 cups hot water
- 1 can (8 oz.) tomato sauce

6 to 8 servings

Prepare spaghetti as directed on package. Rinse and drain. Set aside. In 3-quart casserole, combine sausage, onion, green pepper, chili powder, salt, garlic powder, basil and oregano. Cover. Microwave at High for 6 to 8 minutes, or until vegetables are tender, stirring twice. Stir in spaghetti and remaining ingredients. Microwave, uncovered, at High for 8 to 9 minutes, or until heated through, stirring twice.

New England Clam Chowder

Kandace A. Beale
Kersey, Pennsylvania

2 cups cubed potatoes, ¼-inch cubes
¾ cup thinly sliced celery
1 medium onion, chopped
2 cans (6½ oz. each) minced clams, drained (reserve liquid)
1 teaspoon salt
1 teaspoon dried parsley flakes
¼ teaspoon dried thyme leaves
¼ teaspoon pepper
1 medium carrot, grated
2 cups milk, divided
¼ cup all-purpose flour
3 tablespoons butter or margarine

4 to 6 servings

In 2-quart casserole, combine potatoes, celery, onion, reserved clam liquid, salt, parsley, thyme and pepper. Mix well. Cover. Microwave at High for 5 minutes. Stir in carrot. Re-cover. Microwave at High for 4 to 6 minutes, or until vegetables are tender. In 2-cup measure, blend ¼ cup milk and flour until smooth. Stir flour mixture, remaining 1¾ cups milk and butter into potato mixture. Microwave, uncovered, at High for 5 to 6 minutes, or just until mixture begins to thicken, stirring twice. Stir in clams. Microwave at High for 2 minutes, or until slightly thickened and hot.

Navy Bean Soup

Alva D. Chastain
Annapolis, Maryland

Serve this hot and hearty soup with bread sticks or French bread.

1 lb. dried navy beans, rinsed and sorted
1 large onion, chopped
6 cups hot water
1 ham hock or ham bone
1 medium carrot, grated
1 tablespoon dried celery flakes
1 teaspoon salt
¼ teaspoon pepper
¼ teaspoon dried oregano leaves
⅛ teaspoon dried thyme leaves
1 can (16 oz.) whole tomatoes, cut up
1 cup milk, optional

6 to 8 servings

How to Microwave Navy Bean Soup

Combine beans, onion and water in 5-quart casserole. Cover. Microwave at High for 10 to 15 minutes, or until boiling. Let stand, covered, for 1 hour.

Add ham hock, carrot, celery flakes, salt, pepper, oregano and thyme. Re-cover. Microwave at High for 5 minutes. Reduce power to 50% (Medium). Microwave for 1 hour, turning ham hock over and stirring after every 20 minutes. Remove ham hock from soup.

Cut ham from bone. Return ham to soup. Discard bone. Stir in tomatoes. Re-cover. Microwave at 50% (Medium) for 1½ to 2 hours, or until beans are tender, stirring once. Blend in milk. Mash beans if thicker soup is desired.

Chinese Orange Salad

Salads

Hot Potato & Endive Salad

Mrs. Cindy Hoelscher
Little Canada, Minnesota

2 cups peeled cubed red potatoes, ½-inch cubes
2 tablespoons water
3 slices bacon, cut up
2 tablespoons chopped onion
2 teaspoons all-purpose flour
½ cup water
3 tablespoons vinegar
1 tablespoon sugar
¾ teaspoon salt
2 cups trimmed and torn curly endive (chicory)
2 hard-cooked eggs, sliced

4 to 6 servings

How to Microwave Hot Potato & Endive Salad

Combine potatoes and 2 tablespoons water in 1-quart casserole. Cover. Microwave at High for 4 to 6 minutes, or until tender, stirring once or twice. Drain. Set aside.

Place bacon in same casserole. Cover. Microwave at High for 3 to 4 minutes, or until crisp, stirring once. Remove bacon with slotted spoon onto paper towel. Set aside. Reserve bacon fat.

Stir onion into bacon fat. Re-cover. Microwave at High for 1 minute. Stir in flour.

Blend in ½ cup water, vinegar, sugar and salt. Microwave, uncovered, at High for 2 to 3 minutes, or until mixture thickens and bubbles, stirring once.

Stir in potatoes and bacon. Set aside. Place endive in medium salad bowl.

Pour potato mixture over endive. Toss to coat. Top with egg slices. Serve immediately.

Zucchini Salad

Deborah D. Lathum
Highland, Indiana

6 cups sliced zucchini, ¼ inch
   thick, about 2 lbs.
¼ cup water
¼ cup olive oil
2 tablespoons white wine
   vinegar
1 teaspoon salt
½ to 1 teaspoon white pepper
½ teaspoon sugar
   Salad greens
¼ cup grated Parmesan
   cheese

6 servings

In 2-quart casserole, combine zucchini and water. Cover. Micro-wave at High for 6 to 8 minutes, or until zucchini is tender-crisp, stirring twice. Drain. Set aside. In 1-cup measure, blend olive oil, vinegar, salt, white pepper and sugar.

Pour oil and vinegar mixture over zucchini. Re-cover. Chill for 4 to 5 hours, stirring occasionally. Serve on salad greens. Sprinkle with Parmesan cheese.

Asparagus Vinaigrette

Marilyn Mancewicz
Grand Rapids, Michigan

2 lbs. fresh asparagus spears,
   trimmed and large scales
   removed
¼ cup water
½ cup vegetable oil
2 tablespoons vinegar
2 tablespoons lemon juice
½ teaspoon salt
½ teaspoon Worcestershire
   sauce
½ cup chopped fresh
   mushrooms
2 hard-cooked egg yolks,
   mashed
2 tablespoons sliced
   pimiento-stuffed olives
1 tablespoon snipped fresh
   parsley

4 servings

Arrange asparagus with tender
tips toward center of 10-inch
square casserole. Add water.
Cover. Microwave at High for 8
to 12 minutes, or until asparagus is tender-crisp, rearranging
spears once. Drain. Set aside.

In 2-cup measure, blend oil,
vinegar, lemon juice, salt and
Worcestershire sauce. Microwave at High for 1½ to 2
minutes, or until mixture boils.
Stir in mushrooms, egg yolks,
olives and parsley. Arrange
asparagus on serving platter.
Pour oil and vinegar mixture
over asparagus. Cover with
plastic wrap. Chill for at least
4 hours before serving.

Marinated Vegetables ▲

Margaret Houghtaling
Seattle, Washington

1 cup diagonally sliced carrots,
   ¼ inch thick
1 cup fresh broccoli flowerets
1 cup fresh cauliflowerets
½ cup green pepper pieces,
   1-inch pieces
1 small onion, thinly sliced
1 clove garlic, minced
¼ cup water

1 pkg. (8 oz.) fresh
   mushrooms, halved
⅔ cup white vinegar
½ cup vegetable oil
2 teaspoons salt
2 teaspoons dried basil
   leaves
1½ teaspoons sugar
¼ teaspoon pepper

6 to 8 servings

In 2-quart casserole, combine carrots, broccoli, cauliflower, green
pepper, onion, garlic and water. Cover. Microwave at High for 4 to
5 minutes, or just until colors brighten, stirring once. Stir in mushrooms. Set aside. In small mixing bowl, blend remaining ingredients.
Pour vinegar and oil mixture over vegetables. Mix gently. Chill for
at least 8 hours or overnight, stirring occasionally.

Chinese Orange Salad

Nancy D. Halferty
Broken Bow, Nebraska

A colorful accompaniment to an Oriental stir-fry.

6 cups trimmed and torn mixed salad greens (romaine, leaf or iceberg lettuce, spinach)
3 small navel oranges, peeled, white membrane removed, cut into thin crosswise slices
½ cup sliced celery, ¼ inch thick
2 tablespoons sliced green onion
⅓ cup whole blanched almonds
¼ cup vegetable oil, divided
2 tablespoons sugar
2 tablespoons white rice vinegar
⅛ teaspoon almond extract

6 to 8 servings

In large salad bowl, combine salad greens, oranges, celery and green onion. Set aside. In 9-inch round baking dish or pie plate, combine almonds and 1 tablespoon oil. Microwave at High for 3½ to 5½ minutes, or just until almonds begin to brown, stirring after every minute. Set aside. In 2-cup measure, mix remaining 3 tablespoons oil, sugar, rice vinegar and almond extract. Microwave at High for 1 to 1½ minutes, or until mixture boils. Pour hot mixture over salad. Toss to coat. Mix in toasted almonds.

Zesty Potato Salad ▲

Barbara Bronken
Bozeman, Montana

4 cups peeled cubed red potatoes, ¾-inch cubes
2 tablespoons water
¼ cup finely chopped green pepper
¼ cup chopped onion
2 hard-cooked eggs, chopped
1 tablespoon diced pimiento, drained
1 tablespoon chopped black olives

Dressing:
½ cup mayonnaise
¼ cup salad dressing
1 tablespoon prepared horseradish
1 teaspoon prepared mustard
¾ teaspoon salt
⅛ teaspoon pepper

4 to 6 servings

In 1½-quart casserole, combine potatoes and water. Cover. Microwave at High for 7 to 10 minutes, or until tender, stirring once or twice. Chill for at least 2 hours. Stir in green pepper, onion, eggs, pimiento and olives. In small mixing bowl, blend all dressing ingredients. Pour dressing over salad. Mix well. Re-cover. Chill for at least 3 hours.

Shrimp Salad
with Remoulade Sauce

Myra C. Brooks
Port Allen, Louisiana

1 lb. large shrimp, shelled and
  deveined

Remoulade Sauce:
⅔ cup olive oil
⅓ cup Dijon mustard
¼ cup catsup
¼ cup vinegar
 2 tablespoons prepared
   horseradish
 2 cloves garlic, minced
½ teaspoon hot pepper sauce
¼ teaspoon salt
 2 teaspoons sugar

 4 cups shredded lettuce
½ cup sliced celery, ¼ inch
   thick

4 servings

How to Microwave Shrimp Salad with Remoulade Sauce

Place shrimp in 1½-quart casserole. Set aside. In 2-cup measure, blend all Remoulade Sauce ingredients, except sugar. Pour ¾ cup Remoulade Sauce over shrimp. Stir to coat. Cover. Chill for 1 hour.

Stir sugar into remaining sauce. Cover. Chill. For shrimp, microwave covered at 70% (Medium High) for 5½ to 8 minutes, or until shrimp are opaque, stirring twice. Drain. Place on serving platter. Cover with plastic wrap. Chill for at least 3 hours.

Place lettuce on salad plates. Arrange shrimp and celery on lettuce. Serve with reserved Remoulade Sauce.

Relishes

Pickled Garden Relish

Joan M. Romero
Los Angeles, California

- 3 cups fresh cauliflowerets,
  1-inch pieces
- 2 medium carrots, cut into
  2 × ¼-inch strips
- ¼ cup water
- 1 medium red pepper, cut into
  2 × ¼-inch strips
- 2 stalks celery, sliced ½ inch
  thick
- ⅔ cup whole green or black
  olives
- ¾ cup white wine vinegar
- ½ cup olive oil
- 2 tablespoons sugar
- 1 teaspoon salt
- ½ teaspoon dried oregano
  leaves
- ¼ teaspoon pepper

About 6 cups

In 1½-quart casserole, combine cauliflower, carrots and water. Cover. Microwave at High for 3 to 5 minutes, or until vegetables are hot, but still crisp, stirring once. Stir in red pepper, celery and olives. Set aside.

In 2-cup measure, blend vinegar, olive oil, sugar, salt, oregano and pepper. Pour vinegar and oil mixture over vegetables. Mix well. Re-cover. Chill for at least 8 hours or overnight. Drain before serving.

Cranberry Chutney ▶

Kathy Ferguson
Walnut Creek, California

A traditional family recipe for holidays.

- 1 lb. frozen cranberries
- 1 cup granulated sugar
- ½ cup packed brown sugar
- ½ cup golden raisins
- 2½ teaspoons apple pie spice
- ¾ cup water
- 1 cup peeled chopped pear
- ⅔ cup chopped onion
- ½ cup chopped celery
- ⅓ cup chopped green pepper

4 cups

In 3-quart casserole, combine cranberries, granulated and brown sugars, raisins and apple pie spice. Stir in water. Cover. Microwave at High for 10 to 14 minutes, or until cranberries begin to open, stirring once or twice. Stir in remaining ingredients. Microwave, uncovered, at High for 22 to 30 minutes, or until mixture is desired consistency, stirring 2 or 3 times. Mixture can be stored in refrigerator or ladled into 2 hot sterilized pint jars. Seal and process according to canning directions. Serve as a relish with all meats.

Pepper Jelly

Doyle Henson
Blytheville, Arkansas

Complements the flavor of cooked meats.

- ½ small red pepper
- ½ small green pepper
- 2 seeded fresh jalapeño peppers, each 2½ inches
- 3 cups sugar
- ¾ cup white vinegar
- 1 pouch (3 oz.) liquid fruit pectin

3 cups

In food processor or blender bowl, combine red, green and jalapeño peppers. Process until finely chopped, stopping to scrape side of bowl if needed. Pour mixture into 2-quart measure. Stir in sugar and vinegar. Microwave at High for 5 minutes. Stir thoroughly to dissolve sugar. Microwave at High for 4½ to 6½ minutes, or until mixture comes to a full rolling boil. Microwave at High for 1 minute longer. Add pectin. Mix well. Mixture can be stored in refrigerator or ladled into hot sterilized jars. Seal and process according to canning directions. Serve with all meats.

Shrimp & Scallop Stir-fry

Beef

◄ Pepper Steak

Betty Newlin Harwood
Elgin, Illinois

1½ lbs. beef top round steak,
 ½ inch thick
1 large onion, thinly sliced
1 clove garlic, minced
1½ teaspoons instant beef
 bouillon granules
½ cup water
3 tablespoons soy sauce
2 tablespoons sherry
1 tablespoon cornstarch
2 teaspoons sugar
1 large green pepper, cut into
 8 pieces
1 large red pepper, cut into
 8 pieces

4 to 6 servings

Trim steak and cut into serving-size pieces. Pound to ¼-inch thickness. Arrange pieces in 10-inch square casserole. Top with onion and garlic. Sprinkle with bouillon. In 2-cup measure, combine water, soy sauce and sherry. Blend in cornstarch and sugar. Pour evenly over steak. Cover. Microwave at High for 5 minutes. Reduce power to 50% (Medium). Microwave for 40 minutes to 1 hour, or until beef is tender, turning pieces over once or twice. Add peppers. Microwave at 50% (Medium) for 10 to 15 minutes, or until peppers are tender-crisp, stirring once. Serve with hot cooked rice.

Betty's Pot Roast

June M. Garre
Scottsdale, Arizona

3 to 3½-lb. beef chuck roast
1 cup chopped carrots
1 clove garlic, minced
½ cup red wine
½ cup water
¼ cup catsup
¼ cup soy sauce

Gravy:
¼ cup all-purpose flour
¼ cup water

6 to 8 servings

Place roast in 10-inch square casserole. Sprinkle with carrots. In small mixing bowl, combine garlic, wine, water, catsup and soy sauce. Mix well. Pour over roast. Cover. Microwave at 50% (Medium) for 1 hour 20 minutes to 1 hour 50 minutes, or until tender, turning roast over after half the time. Place roast on serving platter. Cover. Let stand while preparing gravy.

Skim fat from drippings. In 1-cup measure, blend flour and water. Pour into drippings. Microwave at High for 3 to 4 minutes, or until mixture thickens and bubbles, stirring after every minute.

Susan's Chili

Susan B. McIrvin
Jacksonville, North Carolina

Some like it hot.

1 large onion, chopped
1 clove garlic, minced
1½ lbs. lean ground beef
2 cans (16 oz. each) stewed
 tomatoes
2 cans (15 oz. each) kidney
 beans
½ cup ready-to-serve beef
 broth
2½ tablespoons chili powder
1 tablespoon Worcestershire
 sauce
1 teaspoon sugar
1 teaspoon seasoned salt
1 teaspoon ground cumin
1 teaspoon dried oregano
 leaves
¼ teaspoon cayenne
¼ teaspoon pepper

6 to 8 servings

In 3-quart casserole, combine onion and garlic. Cover. Microwave at High for 3 to 4 minutes, or until onion is tender. Crumble beef into onion mixture. Re-cover. Microwave at High for 6 to 8 minutes, or until beef is no longer pink, stirring twice to break apart. Drain. Stir in remaining ingredients. Microwave, uncovered, at High for 10 minutes. Stir. Reduce power to 50% (Medium). Microwave for 20 to 30 minutes, or until flavors are blended, stirring 2 or 3 times.

41

Beef-topped
Twice Baked Potatoes

Brenda Lee Moser
West Lawn, Pennsylvania

- 4 slices bacon
- 4 medium baking potatoes
  (8 oz. each)
- 1 cup water
- 1 pkg. (.87 oz.) beef gravy
  mix
- ¼ teaspoon dried marjoram
  leaves
- ⅛ teaspoon pepper
- 1 lb. boneless beef sirloin
  steak, trimmed and cut
  into thin strips
- 3 to 4 tablespoons milk
- 1 tablespoon butter or
  margarine
- ½ cup finely shredded
  Cheddar cheese

4 servings

How to Microwave Beef-topped Twice Baked Potatoes

Arrange bacon on roasting rack. Cover with paper towel. Microwave at High for 3½ to 4½ minutes, or until brown and crisp. Cool slightly. Crumble. Set aside. Pierce potatoes with fork.

Arrange in circular pattern on paper towel in microwave oven. Microwave at High for 10 to 14 minutes, or until tender, turning potatoes over and rearranging after half the time. Wrap each potato in foil. Set aside.

Blend water, gravy mix, marjoram and pepper in 1-quart casserole. Microwave at High for 4½ to 5½ minutes, or until mixture thickens and bubbles, stirring 2 or 3 times with whisk. Stir in sirloin strips. Microwave at High for 3 to 4 minutes, or until beef is no longer pink, stirring once. Cover. Set aside.

Cut thin slice from top of each potato. Scoop out pulp, leaving about ¼-inch shell. Place pulp in medium mixing bowl.

Arrange shells on large plate. Set aside. Add milk and butter to potato pulp. Beat with electric mixer until smooth and fluffy. Stir in bacon and cheese.

Spoon mixture into potato shells. Microwave at High for 3 to 4 minutes, or until heated through, rotating plate once. Heat gravy and sirloin strips if needed. Serve sirloin and gravy over potatoes.

◄ Enchilada Casserole

Joyce A. Kopsack
Pittsford, Vermont

1 medium onion, chopped
1 pkg. (1.5 oz.) enchilada seasoning mix
1 lb. lean ground beef
1 cup tomato juice
1 can (6 oz.) tomato paste
1 can (4 oz.) chopped green chilies, drained
2 to 3 cups coarsely crushed taco shells or corn chips
2 cups shredded Monterey Jack cheese

6 to 8 servings

Place onion in 1-quart casserole. Cover. Microwave at High for 3 to 4 minutes, or until tender. Stir in enchilada seasoning mix. Crumble beef over onion mixture. Re-cover. Microwave at High for 4 to 6 minutes, or until beef is no longer pink, stirring once to break apart. Stir in tomato juice, tomato paste and green chilies.

Layer half of crushed taco shells, half of meat mixture and half of cheese in 2-quart casserole. Repeat once. Cover with wax paper. Microwave at 70% (Medium High) for 6 to 11 minutes, or until heated through, rotating casserole once.

Pizza Steak

Dawn M. Bendixen
Clear Lake, Wisconsin

2 lbs. beef top round steak, ½ inch thick
1 can (16 oz.) whole tomatoes, drained and cut up
1 can (15 oz.) tomato sauce
1 small onion, finely chopped
1 tablespoon dried parsley flakes

1 teaspoon salt
½ teaspoon dried oregano leaves
⅛ teaspoon garlic powder
⅛ teaspoon pepper
¾ cup shredded mozzarella cheese or ¼ cup grated Parmesan cheese

6 to 8 servings

Trim steak and cut into serving-size pieces. Arrange pieces in 10-inch square casserole. In small mixing bowl, combine remaining ingredients, except cheese. Mix well. Pour evenly over steak. Cover. Microwave at High for 5 minutes. Reduce power to 50% (Medium). Microwave for 55 minutes to 1 hour 10 minutes, or until beef is tender, rearranging pieces twice. Top with cheese. Let stand, covered, for 5 minutes.

Calzone

A restaurant favorite that can be frozen, too.

Nancy J. Klein
Eugene, Oregon

1 lb. loaf frozen bread dough
½ lb. lean ground beef
½ lb. Italian sausage
1 cup sliced fresh mushrooms
½ cup chopped green pepper
¼ cup sliced black olives
¼ cup chopped onion
2 teaspoons Italian seasoning
2 tablespoons catsup
2 cups mozzarella cheese

4 servings

Grease 8 × 4-inch loaf dish. Butter frozen dough on all sides. Place in prepared dish. Microwave at 50% (Medium) for 2 minutes, rotating dish after half the time. Let stand for 5 minutes. Turn dough over. Microwave at 50% (Medium) for 1 to 2 minutes, or until soft to the touch and slightly warm. Cover with plastic wrap. Let rise in warm place until doubled, about 1 hour.

In 2-quart casserole, crumble beef and sausage. Stir in mushrooms, green pepper, olives, onion and Italian seasoning. Cover. Microwave at High for 4 to 6 minutes, or until meat is no longer pink, stirring once to break apart. Drain. Stir in catsup. Set aside.

Preheat conventional oven to 400°F. Lightly oil baking sheet. Set aside. Punch down dough. Divide into 4 equal pieces. Roll or stretch each piece into 8 × 6-inch oval. Place one-fourth of meat mixture in center of each oval. Top with one-fourth of cheese. Fold half of dough over meat and cheese. Seal edges. Repeat with remaining dough. Place on prepared baking sheet. Brush calzones with oil. Bake until lightly browned, 10 to 15 minutes.

Swedish Kaldomars ▶

Thelma L. Williams
Aurora, Illinois

1 medium head cabbage,
    about 2 lbs.
¼ cup water
1 lb. lean ground beef
½ lb. ground pork
1 cup cooked rice
½ cup milk
1 small onion, chopped
1 egg, beaten
1 teaspoon sugar
½ teaspoon salt
½ teaspoon pepper
¼ teaspoon ground allspice
3 tablespoons butter or
    margarine
1 can (16 oz.) whole tomatoes,
    drained and chopped
⅓ cup ready-to-serve beef
    broth

4 to 6 servings

How to Microwave Swedish Kaldomars

Remove core from cabbage. In 5-quart casserole, combine cabbage and water. Cover. Microwave at High for 5 to 7 minutes, or until leaves soften. Let stand, covered, for 5 minutes. Carefully remove 10 outer leaves.

Cut hard center rib from bottom of each leaf. Reserve leaves. In medium mixing bowl, combine beef, pork, rice, milk, onion, egg, sugar, salt, pepper and allspice. Mix well. Place about ⅓ cup meat mixture in center of each leaf.

Fold edges of leaf over, completely enclosing filling. In medium skillet, melt butter over medium-high heat.

Chinese Hamburger Hash

Patricia L. Larabee
Bellflower, California

½ cup chopped celery
½ cup grated carrot
1 medium onion, chopped
½ lb. lean ground beef
1 can (10¾ oz.) condensed
　　cream of mushroom soup
1 cup hot water
½ cup uncooked instant rice
2 tablespoons soy sauce
⅛ teaspoon pepper

4 to 6 servings

In 1½-quart casserole, combine celery, carrot and onion. Cover. Microwave at High for 4 to 6 minutes, or until tender, stirring once. Crumble beef over vegetables. Re-cover. Microwave at High for 2½ to 4 minutes, or until beef is no longer pink, stirring once to break apart. Stir in remaining ingredients. Re-cover. Microwave at High for 8 to 10 minutes, or until rice is tender. Let stand, covered, for 3 to 5 minutes. Serve over crisp Chinese noodles.

Place cabbage rolls in skillet, seam-side down. Brown lightly on both sides. Remove from heat. Place cabbage rolls in 2-quart casserole.

Stir tomatoes and broth into drippings in skillet. Pour over cabbage rolls. Cover.

Microwave at High for 10 to 15 minutes, rotating casserole after every 5 minutes, or until meat is no longer pink and temperature registers 165°F in center of cabbage rolls.

Easy Beef Stew ▲

Juanita Canfield
Seattle, Washington

1 lb. beef stew meat, cut into
   1-inch pieces
1½ cups water
1 cup sliced carrots
1 cup sliced celery
1 cup cubed potatoes,
   ¾-inch cubes
1 large onion, sliced
1 cup tomato juice
2 tablespoons small pearl
   tapioca
1 teaspoon salt
1 teaspoon sugar
½ teaspoon bouquet garni
   seasoning

4 servings

In 3-quart casserole, combine
all ingredients. Mix well. Cover.
Microwave at High for 5 minutes. Reduce power to 50%
(Medium). Microwave for 1½ to
1¾ hours, stirring after every 30
minutes. Let stand, covered, for
10 minutes.

Bev's Meatball Stew

1 lb. lean ground beef
1 pkg. (10 oz.) frozen mixed
   vegetables
1 cup shredded cabbage
½ cup uncooked long grain
   white rice
½ cup medium pearl barley
½ cup chopped celery
1 medium onion, chopped

Mrs. Beverly Goodmund
Blomkest, Minnesota

1 can (14½ oz.) ready-to-serve
   beef broth
1 can (10¾ oz.) condensed
   tomato soup
1 cup water
1 to 2 tablespoons snipped
   fresh parsley
½ teaspoon salt
¼ teaspoon pepper

6 to 8 servings

Shape beef into 18 meatballs, about 1¼ inches each. Set aside.
In 3-quart casserole, combine remaining ingredients. Mix well. Add
meatballs. Cover. Microwave at High for 10 minutes. Stir. Reduce
power to 70% (Medium High). Microwave for 20 to 30 minutes, or
until rice and barley are tender, stirring 2 or 3 times. Let stand,
covered, for 10 minutes.

Stuffed Pepper Soup

Deborah Allegra
North Syracuse, New York

A variation of grandmother's recipe.

3 cups hot water
¾ lb. beef stew meat, cut into
    ½-inch pieces
1 can (8 oz.) whole tomatoes,
    cut up
1 cup sliced carrots, ¼ inch
    thick
½ cup sliced celery, ¼ inch
    thick
½ cup chopped onion
1 tablespoon instant beef
    bouillon granules
1 teaspoon salt, divided
½ teaspoon pepper, divided
½ teaspoon dried parsley
    flakes
4 medium green peppers
½ lb. lean ground beef
⅔ cup uncooked instant rice

4 servings

How to Microwave Stuffed Pepper Soup

Combine water, stew meat, tomatoes, carrots, celery, onion, bouillon, ½ teaspoon salt, ¼ teaspoon pepper and parsley in 3-quart casserole. Cover. Microwave at High for 5 minutes. Reduce power to 50% (Medium). Microwave for 30 minutes.

Cut ½-inch slice from top of each pepper. Remove seeds. Reserve pepper tops. Remove thin slice from bottom of peppers so they will stand upright. Set aside. In small mixing bowl, combine ground beef, rice, remaining ½ teaspoon salt and remaining ¼ teaspoon pepper.

Stuff peppers loosely with rice mixture. Stir soup. Arrange stuffed peppers upright in soup. Place reserved pepper tops on stuffed peppers. Re-cover. Microwave at 50% (Medium) for 30 minutes to 1 hour, or until stew meat is tender, rotating casserole once after 15 minutes. Serve in shallow soup bowls.

Spaghetti Sauce

Linda Henly
Dallas, Texas

Favorite ingredients have been added to prepared spaghetti sauce.

½ lb. lean ground beef
1 tablespoon finely chopped onion
2 cloves garlic, minced
1 jar (32 oz.) spaghetti sauce
1 can (4 oz.) mushroom pieces and stems, drained
2 to 4 tablespoons sherry, optional
1 tablespoon dried parsley flakes
¼ teaspoon Worcestershire sauce
   Dash to ⅛ teaspoon cayenne
1 large bay leaf

4 to 6 servings

Crumble beef into 2-quart casserole. Add onion and garlic. Cover. Microwave at High for 2 to 3½ minutes, or until beef is no longer pink, stirring once to break apart. Drain. Stir in remaining ingredients. Cover with wax paper. Microwave at High for 20 to 30 minutes, or until flavors are blended, stirring 3 or 4 times. Remove bay leaf. Serve over hot cooked spaghetti.

Mexican Beef-n-Macaroni ▲

Donna Steiner
Omaha, Nebraska

1 cup uncooked elbow macaroni
1 lb. lean ground beef
½ cup chopped onion
½ cup chopped green pepper
1 can (15 oz.) tomato sauce
2 teaspoons chili powder
¾ teaspoon salt
½ to 1 teaspoon ground cumin
⅛ teaspoon pepper

Topping:
1 cup crushed corn chips
½ cup finely shredded Cheddar cheese

4 to 6 servings

Prepare macaroni as directed on package. Rinse and drain. Set aside. Crumble beef into 1½-quart casserole. Stir in onion and green pepper. Cover. Microwave at High for 5 to 8 minutes, or until beef is no longer pink, stirring once to break apart. Drain. Stir in remaining ingredients, except topping. Re-cover. Microwave at High for 8 to 10 minutes, or until flavors are blended, stirring once.

Sprinkle with corn chips and cheese. Microwave at High for 30 seconds to 1 minute, or until cheese melts.

Italian Chili

Kathleen T. Schreiber
Burdett, Kansas

½ lb. lean ground beef
1 medium onion, chopped
½ cup chopped green
   pepper
½ cup chopped celery
1 clove garlic, minced
1 can (28 oz.) whole
   tomatoes, cut up
1 can (15 oz.) kidney beans,
   drained
1½ cups tomato juice

1 can (8 oz.) mushroom
   pieces and stems, drained
1 can (6 oz.) tomato paste
1 pkg. (3½ oz.) sliced
   pepperoni, cut up
1½ teaspoons Italian seasoning
½ teaspoon salt
½ teaspoon sugar
¼ to ½ teaspoon dried
   crushed red pepper

8 to 10 servings

Crumble beef into 3-quart casserole. Stir in onion, green pepper, celery and garlic. Cover. Microwave at High for 5 to 8 minutes, or until beef is no longer pink and vegetables are tender-crisp, stirring once or twice to break apart. Stir in remaining ingredients. Mix well. Re-cover. Microwave at High for 20 minutes, stirring once or twice. Microwave, uncovered, at High for 10 to 15 minutes, or until desired consistency and flavors are blended.

American Lasagne

Gloria Struhelka
Pewaukee, Wisconsin

12 uncooked lasagne noodles

Sauce:

½ lb. lean ground beef
1 clove garlic, minced
1 can (16 oz.) whole tomatoes, drained and chopped
1 can (6 oz.) tomato paste
¾ teaspoon Italian seasoning
½ teaspoon salt
½ teaspoon dried oregano leaves
¼ teaspoon sugar
¼ teaspoon pepper

2 cups small curd cottage cheese
2 eggs
¾ cup grated Parmesan cheese, divided
2 cups shredded mozzarella cheese

6 to 8 servings

How to Microwave American Lasagne

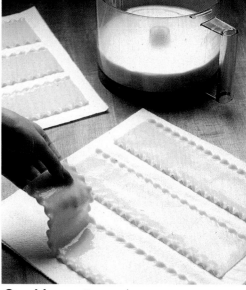

Prepare lasagne noodles as directed on package. Rinse. Let stand in warm water while preparing sauce.

Crumble beef into 1-quart casserole. Add garlic. Cover. Microwave at High for 2 to 3 minutes, or until beef is no longer pink, stirring once to break apart. Drain. Stir in remaining sauce ingredients. Re-cover. Microwave at High for 5 minutes, stirring after half the time. Set aside.

Combine cottage cheese, eggs and ¼ cup Parmesan cheese in food processor or blender bowl. Process until smooth. Set aside. Place lasagne noodles on paper towels to drain.

Layer 4 noodles, half of mozzarella cheese, half of cottage cheese mixture and half of sauce in 10-inch square casserole. Repeat once. Top with remaining 4 noodles. Sprinkle with remaining ½ cup Parmesan cheese.

Cover with vented plastic wrap. Microwave at High for 5 minutes. Rotate casserole half turn. Reduce power to 70% (Medium High).

Microwave for 10 to 14 minutes, or until temperature in center registers 150°F, rotating casserole twice. Let stand, covered, for 10 minutes. Garnish with dried parsley flakes, if desired.

◄ Crazy Mixed-Up Cabbage Bake

Donna R. Roundy
Huber Heights, Ohio

1 medium onion, chopped
1 lb. lean ground beef
½ lb. pork sausage
½ cup uncooked instant rice
½ teaspoon dried majoram leaves
¼ teaspoon dried basil leaves
¼ teaspoon salt
⅛ teaspoon pepper

Tomato Sauce:
1 can (15 oz.) tomato sauce
¼ teaspoon salt
¼ teaspoon sugar
¼ teaspoon dried basil leaves
⅛ teaspoon pepper

1 jar (32 oz.) sauerkraut, drained
5 cups sliced cabbage, ¼ inch thick

6 to 8 servings

Place onion in 1½-quart casserole. Cover. Microwave at High for 3 to 4 minutes, or until tender. Crumble beef and sausage over onion. Re-cover. Microwave at High for 6 to 7 minutes, or until meat is no longer pink, stirring once to break apart. Drain. Stir in rice, marjoram, basil, salt and pepper. Set aside. In small mixing bowl, blend all Tomato Sauce ingredients. Set aside.

In 10-inch square casserole, layer half of sauerkraut, half of cabbage, half of meat mixture and half of tomato sauce. Repeat once. Cover. Microwave at High for 5 minutes. Reduce power to 70% (Medium High). Microwave for 20 to 30 minutes, or until cabbage is tender, rotating casserole once. Let stand, covered, for 5 minutes.

◄ Old-Fashioned Spaghetti & Meatballs

Barbara S. Scholl
Lancaster, Ohio

Meatballs:
1 lb. lean ground beef
¼ lb. lean ground pork
½ cup quick-cooking rolled oats
¼ cup grated Parmesan cheese
¼ cup milk
1 egg, beaten
2 tablespoons snipped fresh parsley
1 clove garlic, minced
½ teaspoon salt
3 tablespoons olive oil

Sauce:
¾ cup chopped onion
⅓ cup chopped celery
1 clove garlic, minced
2 cans (15 oz. each) tomato sauce
1 can (16 oz.) whole tomatoes
1 can (6 oz.) tomato paste
⅓ cup snipped fresh parsley
1 tablespoon packed brown sugar
2 teaspoons dried oregano leaves
2 teaspoons dried basil leaves
½ teaspoon ground allspice
½ teaspoon chili powder
1 bay leaf

6 to 8 servings

In medium mixing bowl, combine all meatball ingredients, except olive oil. Mix well. Shape into 36 meatballs, about 1½ inches each. In large skillet, heat olive oil over medium-high heat. Brown meatballs, about 5 minutes, turning occasionally. Remove from heat. Reserve 2 tablespoons olive oil from skillet in 3-quart casserole. Set aside. Drain meatballs. Set aside.

For sauce, combine onion, celery and garlic with reserved oil in casserole. Cover. Microwave at High for 3 to 6 minutes, or until tender. Stir in remaining sauce ingredients and meatballs. Re-cover. Microwave at High for 10 minutes. Reduce power to 70% (Medium High). Microwave for 20 to 30 minutes, or until flavors are blended, stirring occasionally. Remove bay leaf. Serve over hot cooked spaghetti. Sprinkle with Parmesan cheese, if desired.

Pork

◄ Pork Chops in Wine Sauce

Nancy Elizabeth Harris
Little Falls, New Jersey

1 tablespoon butter or margarine
1 large onion, sliced
2 tablespoons all-purpose flour
¼ teaspoon garlic powder
⅛ teaspoon pepper
4 butterflied pork chops, about ½ inch thick
½ cup white wine
2 tablespoons soy sauce
1 tablespoon snipped fresh parsley, optional

4 servings

In 9-inch square baking dish, combine butter and onion. Cover with plastic wrap. Microwave at High for 3 to 4 minutes, or until onion is tender-crisp. In large plastic food storage bag, combine flour, garlic powder and pepper. Add chops. Shake to coat. Arrange coated chops over onion, adding any excess flour mixture to dish. In 1-cup measure, combine wine and soy sauce. Pour over chops. Cover with plastic wrap. Microwave at High for 3 minutes. Reduce power to 50% (Medium). Microwave for 5 minutes. Turn chops over. Spoon sauce over chops. Re-cover. Microwave at 50% (Medium) for 10 to 15 minutes, or until pork is no longer pink. Let stand, covered, for 3 minutes. Top with parsley.

Marinated Pork Chops

Ronald E. Allen, Sr.
Stone Mountain, Georgia

½ cup catsup
½ cup dark rum
3½ teaspoons chopped fresh chives or 2 teaspoons freeze-dried chives
1 tablespoon dried basil leaves
1 tablespoon chili powder
1 tablespoon hot pepper sauce
½ teaspoon garlic powder or 1 clove garlic, minced
4 pork loin chops (8 oz. each) ¾ inch thick

4 servings

In 4-cup measure, combine all ingredients, except chops. Mix well. Microwave at 50% (Medium) for 3 to 4 minutes, or until hot, stirring once. Cool for 15 to 20 minutes. Arrange chops in 10-inch square casserole. Pour marinade over chops. Turn chops to coat. Cover with plastic wrap. Chill for 3 to 4 hours. Remove chops from marinade. Arrange on roasting rack. Microwave at 70% (Medium High) for 15 to 19 minutes, or until thoroughly cooked, rearranging chops once or twice.

Bavarian Bratwurst Casserole

Debra Swan
Laurel, Montana

2 cups cubed red potatoes, ¾-inch cubes
¼ cup finely chopped onion
¼ cup water
1 can (16 oz.) sauerkraut, drained
¾ lb. uncooked bratwurst, cut into 1-inch pieces
1 medium apple, cored and thinly sliced
2 tablespoons packed brown sugar
1 tablespoon dried parsley flakes
1 tablespoon lemon juice
1 teaspoon caraway seed
2 tablespoons all-purpose flour
1 cup beer, divided

4 servings

In 2-quart casserole, combine potatoes, onion and water. Cover. Microwave at High for 5 to 7 minutes, or until potatoes are tender. Stir in sauerkraut, bratwurst, apple, brown sugar, parsley, lemon juice and caraway. In small bowl, blend flour and ¼ cup beer. Stir in remaining ¾ cup beer. Pour into bratwurst and potato mixture. Mix well. Re-cover. Microwave at High for 9 to 12 minutes, or until bratwurst is firm and no longer pink, stirring 2 or 3 times.

Sausage-Rice Casserole

Dorothy Ahlquist
Fairfield Bay, Arkansas

1 lb. pork sausage
1 medium onion, chopped
1 medium green pepper,
   chopped
2 cans (14½ oz. each)
   ready-to-serve chicken
   broth
1 cup uncooked long grain
   white rice
½ cup uncooked wild rice,
   rinsed and drained
1 can (4 oz.) sliced
   mushrooms, drained
1 teaspoon Italian seasoning
½ teaspoon fennel seed
1 cup shredded Monterey
   Jack cheese

6 to 8 servings

Crumble sausage into 2-quart
casserole. Add onion and green
pepper. Cover. Microwave at
High for 6 to 8 minutes, or until
sausage is no longer pink,
stirring once to break apart.
Drain thoroughly. Set aside.

In 3-quart casserole, combine
broth, white and wild rice,
mushrooms, Italian seasoning
and fennel. Mix well. Cover.
Microwave at High for 8 to 10
minutes, or until broth boils. Stir.
Re-cover. Reduce power to
50% (Medium). Microwave for
30 to 35 minutes, or until rice is
tender and liquid is absorbed.
Stir in sausage mixture. Top with
cheese. Re-cover. Microwave
at 50% (Medium) for 5 to 10
minutes, or until heated through
and cheese melts.

Bacon-Macaroni Bake

Lucile L. Nelson
Baltimore, Maryland

2 cups uncooked elbow
    macaroni
10 slices bacon, cut up
1 can (15 oz.) tomato sauce
1 can (6 oz.) tomato paste
3 tablespoons snipped fresh
    parsley, divided
½ teaspoon sugar
⅛ to ¼ teaspoon garlic powder
⅛ teaspoon pepper
¼ cup grated Parmesan
    cheese

6 to 8 servings

Prepare macaroni as directed
on package. Rinse and drain.
Set aside. Place bacon in
2-quart casserole. Microwave at
High for 4 minutes. Drain and
discard fat. Stir. Microwave at
High for 4 to 7 minutes, or until
bacon is crisp. Drain, reserving
1 tablespoon fat in casserole.
Stir in tomato sauce, tomato
paste, 2 tablespoons parsley,
sugar, garlic powder and
pepper. Mix well. Cover. Microwave at High for 8 to 10 minutes,
or until flavors are blended,
stirring once or twice. Stir in
cooked macaroni.

Mix remaining 1 tablespoon
parsley and the cheese in small
bowl. Sprinkle over macaroni
mixture. Re-cover. Microwave
at High for 2 to 3 minutes, or
until hot.

Sweet & Sour Pork ▲

Mrs. Lynn Ann Kennedy
Cinnaminson, New Jersey

Sauce:

¼ cup sugar
4½ teaspoons cornstarch
1 can (8 oz.) pineapple
  chunks, drained
  (reserve juice)
¼ cup soy sauce
3 tablespoons catsup
3 tablespoons vinegar
2 tablespoons white wine
½ teaspoon minced fresh
  gingerroot
  Dash cayenne

1 lb. boneless pork loin or
  tenderloin, cut into ¾-inch
  pieces
1 can (8 oz.) bamboo shoots,
  drained
½ cup cubed green pepper,
  ½-inch cubes
½ cup diagonally sliced
  carrot, ¼ inch thick
1 small onion, cut into
  4 pieces and separated
1 clove garlic, minced

4 to 6 servings

In 4-cup measure, combine sugar and cornstarch. Place reserved pineapple juice in 1-cup measure. Add water to equal ⅔ cup. Stir into sugar and cornstarch. Blend in remaining sauce ingredients, except pineapple chunks. Set aside. Place pork in 2-quart casserole. Cover. Microwave at High for 4 to 6 minutes, or until pork is no longer pink, stirring once. Reserve pork and drippings in medium bowl. Set aside.

In same 2-quart casserole, combine bamboo shoots, green pepper, carrot, onion and garlic. Cover. Microwave at High for 5 to 6 minutes, or until carrot is tender-crisp, stirring once. Set aside. For sauce, microwave at High for 4 to 6 minutes, or until thickened and translucent, stirring twice. Pour sauce over vegetables. Stir in pork and pineapple chunks. Mix well. Microwave at High for 2 minutes, or until heated through. Serve over hot cooked rice.

Hungarian Pork Stew

Patricia Wolfe
Clearwater, Florida

2 tablespoons all-purpose
  flour
1½ to 2 lbs. pork stew meat,
  cut into ¾-inch pieces
1 jar (32 oz.) sauerkraut,
  rinsed and drained
1 large onion, finely chopped
2 tablespoons paprika
1 teaspoon sugar
1 teaspoon caraway seed
¼ teaspoon pepper
2 bay leaves
2 cups hot water
1 cup dairy sour cream

6 to 8 servings

In large plastic food storage bag, combine flour and pork. Shake to coat. Place in 3-quart casserole. Stir in remaining ingredients, except sour cream. Cover. Microwave at High for 5 minutes. Reduce power to 50% (Medium). Microwave for 50 minutes to 1 hour 10 minutes, or until pork is tender, stirring once or twice. Remove bay leaves. Stir in sour cream.

Pork Roast & Gravy

Charlotte D. Eufers
San Diego, California

- 2 tablespoons all-purpose flour
- ½ teaspoon seasoned salt
- ¼ teaspoon garlic powder
- 2½ to 3-lb. boneless pork loin roast
- ¼ cup water
- ¼ cup Worcestershire sauce
- 2 teaspoons whole peppercorns

Gravy:

- 1 can (4 oz.) sliced mushrooms, drained
- 2 tablespoons all-purpose flour
- ½ cup water
- ¼ teaspoon bouquet sauce

6 to 8 servings

In large oven cooking bag, combine flour, seasoned salt and garlic powder. Add roast, water, Worcestershire sauce and peppercorns. Tie bag loosely with string or nylon tie. Place in 9-inch square baking dish. Estimate total cooking time at 17 to 20 minutes per pound. Divide total cooking time in half. Microwave at High for first 5 minutes. Reduce power to 50% (Medium). Microwave the remainder of first half of time. Turn roast over. Microwave at 50% (Medium) for second half of time, or until internal temperature registers 165°F in several places, rotating dish once or twice. Place roast on serving platter. Cover. Let stand while preparing gravy.

Strain drippings into 4-cup measure. Skim fat from surface. Add water to equal ¾ cup liquid. Stir in mushrooms. In small bowl, blend flour, ½ cup water and bouquet sauce. Stir into mushroom mixture. Microwave at High for 2½ to 4½ minutes, or until mixture thickens and bubbles, stirring twice. Serve gravy over sliced pork roast.

Pork Chops & Green Peppers ▲

Patricia R. McCann
Arvada, Colorado

- ¼ cup all-purpose flour
- ½ teaspoon salt
- ⅛ teaspoon pepper
- 4 pork loin chops (8 oz. each) ¾ inch thick
- 2 tablespoons vegetable oil
- 2 cups hot cooked rice
- 1 medium onion, chopped
- 1 large green pepper, chopped
- 1 cup sliced fresh mushrooms
- 1 can (16 oz.) whole tomatoes, drained and chopped

Gravy:

- 3 tablespoons all-purpose flour
- 1½ cups water, divided
- 1 teaspoon instant chicken bouillon granules
- ½ teaspoon bouquet sauce
- ¼ teaspoon salt
- ⅛ teaspoon pepper

4 servings

In large plastic food storage bag, combine flour, salt and pepper. Add chops. Shake to coat. Set aside. In large skillet, heat oil over medium-high heat. Brown chops on both sides. Set aside. Spread rice evenly over bottom of 10-inch square casserole. Arrange chops on rice. Reserve pan drippings. Sprinkle chops with onion, green pepper and mushrooms. Top with tomatoes. Set aside.

In 1-cup measure, blend flour with ¼ cup water. Stir in bouillon, bouquet sauce, salt and pepper. Pour remaining 1¼ cups water into reserved drippings in skillet. Stir in flour and water mixture. Cook over medium heat until boiling, stirring constantly. Pour gravy over chops. Cover. Microwave at 70% (Medium High) for 25 to 30 minutes, or until pork is no longer pink, rotating casserole twice. Let stand, covered, for 10 minutes.

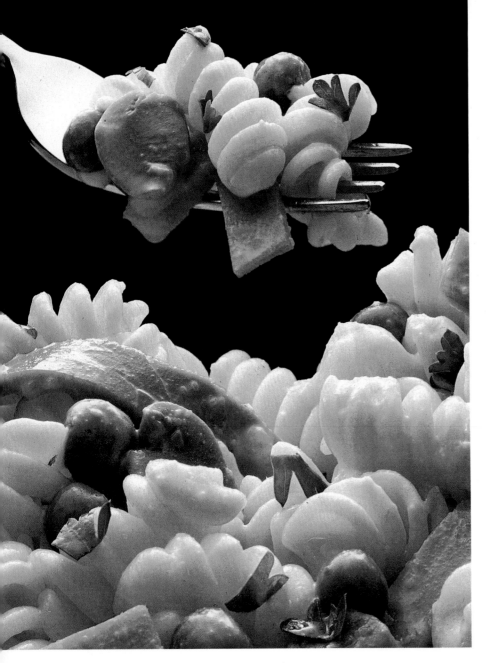

German Stew

Mickey I. Greene
Freemont, Ohio

Other stew meats can be used in this old-fashioned recipe.

- 1 large apple, peeled, cored and shredded
- 1 medium carrot, shredded
- 1 medium onion, sliced
- 1 clove garlic, minced
- 1½ lbs. pork stew meat, cut into ¾-inch pieces
- 1⅓ cups water, divided
- 1 cup beer
- 2 teaspoons instant beef bouillon granules
- ½ teaspoon dried thyme leaves
- ½ teaspoon anchovy paste
- ¼ teaspoon poppy seed
- 1 bay leaf
- 4 teaspoons cornstarch
- ½ teaspoon bouquet sauce

4 to 6 servings

In 3-quart casserole, combine apple, carrot, onion and garlic. Cover. Microwave at High for 3 to 4 minutes, or until carrot is tender. Stir in pork, 1 cup water, beer, bouillon, thyme, anchovy paste, poppy seed and bay leaf. Re-cover. Microwave at High for 5 minutes. Reduce power to 50% (Medium). Microwave for 1 to 1¼ hours, or until pork is tender, stirring twice. Remove bay leaf.

In 1-cup measure, blend cornstarch, remaining ⅓ cup water and bouquet sauce. Stir into hot pork mixture. Microwave at High for 2 to 3 minutes, or until mixture is thickened, stirring once. Serve stew over hot cooked egg noodles.

Ham & Rotini ▲

Cheryl A. Kirkpatrick
Bear, Delaware

- 8 oz. uncooked rotini pasta
- ¼ cup butter or margarine
- ¾ lb. fully cooked ham, cut into 2 × ¼-inch strips
- 1 cup frozen peas
- ½ cup grated Parmesan cheese
- ½ cup whipping cream
- 1 can (4 oz.) sliced mushrooms, drained
- 1 egg, slightly beaten
- 1 tablespoon snipped fresh parsley

4 servings

Prepare rotini as directed on package. Rinse and drain. Set aside. Place butter in 2-quart casserole. Microwave at High for 1¼ to 1½ minutes, or until butter melts. Stir in ham, peas, cheese, cream, mushrooms, egg and parsley. Stir in rotini. Cover. Microwave at High for 5 to 7 minutes, or until heated through, stirring twice.

Cajun Gumbo

Amanda Greene
Marshall, Texas

- 1 large onion, chopped
- 10 thin slices seeded fresh jalapeño pepper, optional
- 1 clove garlic, minced
- ¾ lb. hot pork sausage
- 1 can (16 oz.) stewed tomatoes
- 1 cup frozen mixed vegetables
- 1 cup water
- 1 pkg. (6 oz.) frozen sliced okra
- ½ cup cubed fully cooked ham, ½-inch cubes
- 1 tablespoon chili powder
- 1 teaspoon salt
- ⅛ teaspoon pepper
- 2 cans (16 oz. each) black-eyed peas, drained

8 to 10 servings

In 3-quart casserole, combine onion, jalapeño pepper and garlic. Cover. Microwave at High for 4 to 5 minutes, or until onion is tender, stirring once. Crumble sausage over onion mixture. Re-cover. Microwave at High for 4 to 5 minutes, or until sausage is no longer pink, stirring once to break apart. Drain. Stir in tomatoes, mixed vegetables, water, okra, ham, chili powder, salt and pepper. Re-cover. Microwave at High for 15 to 20 minutes, or until flavors are blended, stirring twice. Stir in black-eyed peas. Re-cover. Microwave at High for 3 minutes, or until heated through. Serve over hot cooked rice.

Lamb

Spinach-stuffed Lamb

Judith Hackler
Elkins Park, Pennsylvania

5-lb. boneless leg of lamb,
  rolled and tied
1 tablespoon curry powder
1 teaspoon pepper
1 teaspoon minced fresh garlic
½ teaspoon ground ginger
½ lb. fresh spinach, trimmed,
  stems removed

Stuffing:
⅓ cup butter or margarine
2 cups soft raisin bread
  crumbs (4 to 5 slices)
¼ cup sliced green onions
1 tablespoon snipped fresh
  parsley
¼ teaspoon pepper

10 to 12 servings

How to Microwave Spinach-stuffed Lamb

Untie lamb and lay flat on work surface. Remove any large fat deposits. In small bowl, combine curry powder, pepper, garlic and ginger. Mix well. Rub over inside of lamb surface. Layer spinach over lamb. Set aside.

Place butter in small mixing bowl. Microwave at High for 1½ to 1¾ minutes, or until butter melts. Stir in remaining ingredients. Spread stuffing mixture over spinach. Re-roll lamb, enclosing spinach and stuffing.

Tie securely. Place on roasting rack. Microwave at High for 8 minutes. Turn lamb over. Reduce power to 50% (Medium). Microwave for 37 to 57 minutes, or until internal temperature in center registers 135 to 140°F for medium doneness, turning lamb over after half the time. Let stand, tented with foil, for 10 minutes before carving.

Gyros Loaf

Delicious served warm or cold.

Betty Newlin Harwood
Elgin, Illinois

Gyros Loaf:

- 2 slices white bread, torn into small pieces
- ¼ cup water
- ½ lb. ground lamb
- ½ lb. lean ground beef
- 1 egg, beaten
- ¼ cup finely chopped onion
- 1½ teaspoons dried parsley flakes
- 1½ teaspoons dried oregano leaves
- 1½ teaspoons dried mint flakes
- ¾ teaspoon salt
- ⅛ teaspoon pepper
- 1 clove garlic, minced

Yogurt-Cucumber Sauce:

- 1 container (8 oz.) plain low-fat yogurt
- 1 small onion, sliced and separated into rings
- ½ cup peeled, seeded and finely chopped cucumber
- 1 tablespoon snipped fresh parsley, optional
- 1½ teaspoons lemon juice
- ¼ teaspoon salt
- 6 to 8 pita breads, 6-inch, cut in half
  Lettuce, optional
  Chopped tomatoes, optional

6 to 8 servings

In large mixing bowl, combine bread and water. Let stand for 3 minutes. Mix. Stir in remaining loaf ingredients. Shape into loaf. Place in 8 × 4-inch loaf dish. Place on saucer in microwave oven. Microwave at 70% (Medium High) for 19 to 24 minutes, or until internal temperature in center registers 150°F, rotating dish twice. Let stand for 10 minutes. Drain thoroughly. Slice. Set aside.

In small mixing bowl, blend all sauce ingredients. Place slices of Gyros Loaf in each pita bread. Serve with lettuce and tomatoes. Spoon Yogurt-Cucumber Sauce over each pita.

Veal

Italian Veal & Rice

Clara G. DeRose
Bloomsburg, Pennsylvania

- 2 tablespoons olive oil
- 1 lb. veal round steak, trimmed, cut into ½-inch cubes
- 2 Italian frying peppers or 1 medium green pepper, cut into thin strips
- 8 oz. sliced fresh mushrooms
- 1 medium onion, thinly sliced
- 2 cloves garlic, minced
- ½ teaspoon Italian seasoning
- 1 can (16 oz.) whole tomatoes
- 1½ cups uncooked instant rice
- 1 cup frozen Italian green beans
- ⅔ cup white wine or chicken broth
- 1 teaspoon salt
- ¼ teaspoon pepper

4 to 6 servings

Preheat 10-inch browning dish at High for 5 minutes. Quickly add olive oil and veal. Stir until sizzling stops. Stir in peppers, mushrooms, onion, garlic and Italian seasoning. Cover. Microwave at High for 6 to 10 minutes, or just until vegetables are tender, stirring once or twice. Add remaining ingredients. Stir well. Re-cover. Microwave at High for 6 to 8 minutes, or until hot and bubbly, stirring once. Let stand, covered, for 5 minutes, or until rice is tender. Stir with fork before serving.

Veal & Mushrooms

Joan T. Ellis
Fort Myers, Florida

- 1 teaspoon butter or margarine
- 1 teaspoon olive oil
- 8 oz. fresh mushrooms, thinly sliced
- 1 cup chopped onion
- 2 tablespoons snipped fresh parsley, divided
- 1 clove garlic, minced
- 1 cup ready-to-serve chicken broth
- ½ teaspoon salt
- ¼ teaspoon pepper
- 1½ lbs. veal stew meat, cut into 1¼-inch pieces
- ¼ cup all-purpose flour
- 2 eggs, beaten
- ½ cup seasoned dry bread crumbs
- 1 cup dairy sour cream

4 to 6 servings

In 2-quart casserole, combine butter, olive oil, mushrooms, onion, 1 tablespoon parsley and garlic. Cover. Microwave at High for 3 to 4 minutes, or until onion is tender-crisp, stirring once. Stir in broth, salt and pepper. Set aside.

In large plastic food storage bag, combine veal and flour. Shake to coat. Place floured veal in egg, stirring to coat. Lift veal with slotted spoon, allowing excess egg to drain off. Place veal in another large plastic food storage bag. Add bread crumbs. Shake to coat. Stir veal into vegetables and broth. Re-cover. Reduce power to 70% (Medium High). Microwave for 35 to 45 minutes, or until veal is tender, stirring gently twice. Blend in sour cream. Top with remaining 1 tablespoon parsley. Serve over cooked spinach noodles or egg noodles. Sprinkle with Parmesan cheese, if desired. Garnish with tomato rose.

How to Make a Tomato Rose Garnish

Remove tomato skin in thin continuous ¾-inch strip.

Roll strip into a coil, fanning slightly to form a rose.

67

Poultry

◄ Barbecued Chicken

Mrs. Jean Ivy
Oklahoma City, Oklahoma

3 tablespoons chopped onion
2 cloves garlic, minced
2 teaspoons butter or
　margarine
1 can (8 oz.) tomato sauce
¼ cup vinegar
3 tablespoons sugar
2 tablespoons Worcestershire
　sauce
½ teaspoon salt
¼ teaspoon pepper
¼ teaspoon celery seed
⅛ to ¼ teaspoon liquid smoke
2½ to 3-lb. broiler-fryer chicken,
　cut into 8 pieces

4 servings

In 4-cup measure, combine
onion, garlic and butter. Microwave at High for 2 to 3 minutes,
or until onion is tender. Stir in
remaining ingredients, except
chicken. Cover with wax paper.
Microwave at High for 3 minutes.
Stir. Re-cover. Reduce power to
50% (Medium). Microwave for
10 to 15 minutes, or until flavors
are blended, stirring once.
Arrange chicken skin-side down
in 9-inch square baking dish.
Pour half of sauce over chicken.
Cover with wax paper. Microwave at 70% (Medium High) for
10 minutes. Turn pieces over.
Pour remaining sauce over
chicken. Microwave, uncovered,
at 70% (Medium High) for 12 to
18 minutes, or until chicken is
no longer pink and juices run
clear, rearranging pieces once.
Let stand for 3 to 5 minutes.

Pauline's Cheesy Turkey Cutlets

Mrs. Pauline Baluh
Mount Pleasant, Pennsylvania

*Family and friends enjoy this
easy-to-prepare main dish.*

½ cup butter or margarine
2 cups Cheddar cheese
　crackers
1½ teaspoons Mexican
　seasoning
6 turkey cutlets (2 to 3 oz.
　each) ¼ inch thick
1½ cups shredded mozzarella
　cheese

4 to 6 servings

Place butter in medium bowl.
Microwave at High for 1½ to 1¾
minutes, or until butter melts.
Set aside. Place crackers in
food processor or blender bowl.
Process until fine crumbs. Stir in
Mexican seasoning. Dip each
cutlet in melted butter and then
in crumbs to coat, pressing
lightly. Arrange three coated
cutlets in single layer in 9-inch
square baking dish. Sprinkle
with half of mozzarella cheese.
Top with remaining cutlets and
cheese. Sprinkle with remaining
cracker crumbs. Drizzle with
remaining butter. Cover with
wax paper. Microwave at 70%
(Medium High) for 9 to 12
minutes, or until turkey is firm
and no longer pink, rotating
dish after every 3 minutes.

Chicken-in-Beer

Judy A. Baird
Dunkirk, New York

¾ cup beer
¼ cup tomato sauce
1½ teaspoons paprika
¼ teaspoon dried thyme
　leaves
2 small onions, each cut into
　8 pieces
¼ cup all-purpose flour
1 teaspoon salt
⅛ teaspoon pepper
2½ to 3-lb. broiler-fryer chicken,
　cut into 8 pieces
3 tablespoons butter or
　margarine
¼ cup whipping cream

4 servings

In 10-inch square casserole,
combine beer, tomato sauce,
paprika and thyme. Mix well.
Add onions. Set aside.

In large plastic food storage
bag, combine flour, salt and
pepper. Add chicken pieces.
Shake to coat. In large skillet,
melt butter over medium-high
heat. Quickly brown chicken on
both sides. Arrange chicken in
casserole over sauce. Cover.
Microwave at High for 5 minutes.
Reduce power to 50% (Medium).
Microwave for 10 to 15 minutes,
or until chicken is no longer
pink and juices run clear,
rearranging pieces once. Place
chicken on serving platter.
Blend whipping cream into
sauce in casserole. Microwave
at 50% (Medium) for 2 to 3
minutes, or until heated through.
Serve over chicken.

69

Chicken Supreme

Nancy D. Halferty
Broken Bow, Nebraska

Chicken and vegetables make this casserole a family favorite.

- 1 cup uncooked instant rice
- 1 cup shredded carrots
- ½ cup chopped celery
- 2 tablespoons finely chopped onion
- 2 teaspoons dried parsley flakes
- 1 pkg. (10 oz.) frozen asparagus cuts
- 2 whole bone-in chicken breasts (about 1 lb. each) skin removed, split in half
- 1 can (10¾ oz.) condensed cream of celery soup
- 1 cup water
- 2 tablespoons soy sauce
- ⅛ teaspoon pepper
- 1 cup herb seasoned stuffing mix

4 servings

In 10-inch square casserole, combine rice, carrots, celery, onion and parsley. Mix well. Set aside. Unwrap asparagus and place on plate. Microwave at High for 2 to 3 minutes, or until defrosted, stirring after half the time to break apart. Drain. Sprinkle asparagus evenly over rice and vegetable mixture. Arrange chicken over rice. In medium bowl, mix soup, water, soy sauce and pepper. Pour evenly over chicken. Sprinkle with stuffing mix. Cover. Microwave at 70% (Medium High) for 25 to 30 minutes, or until chicken is no longer pink, rotating casserole after every 10 minutes.

Jim's Cashew Chicken Chop Suey

James F. Koby
Lebanon, Missouri

2 boneless whole chicken
   breasts (10 to 12 oz. each)
   skin removed, cut into
   1 × ¼-inch strips
½ cup sliced celery, ¼ inch
   thick
1 small onion, thinly sliced
3 tablespoons soy sauce
1 teaspoon minced fresh
   gingerroot
½ teaspoon salt
⅛ teaspoon pepper
3 tablespoons cornstarch
¼ cup water
1 can (14½ oz.) ready-to-serve
   chicken broth
1 can (14 oz.) bean sprouts,
   drained
1 can (8 oz.) sliced water
   chestnuts, drained
1 can (8 oz.) bamboo shoots,
   drained
1 can (4 oz.) sliced
   mushrooms, drained
½ cup cashews

4 to 6 servings

How to Microwave Jim's Cashew Chicken Chop Suey

Combine chicken, celery, onion, soy sauce, gingerroot, salt and pepper in 2-quart casserole. Mix well. Cover. Microwave at High for 5 to 8 minutes, or until vegetables are tender and chicken is no longer pink, stirring once or twice.

Blend cornstarch and water in 1-cup measure. Stir into vegetables and chicken. Stir in remaining ingredients, except cashews. Microwave, uncovered, at High for 15 to 19 minutes, or until mixture is thickened and translucent, stirring 2 or 3 times.

Serve over crisp Chinese noodles or hot cooked rice. Sprinkle with cashews.

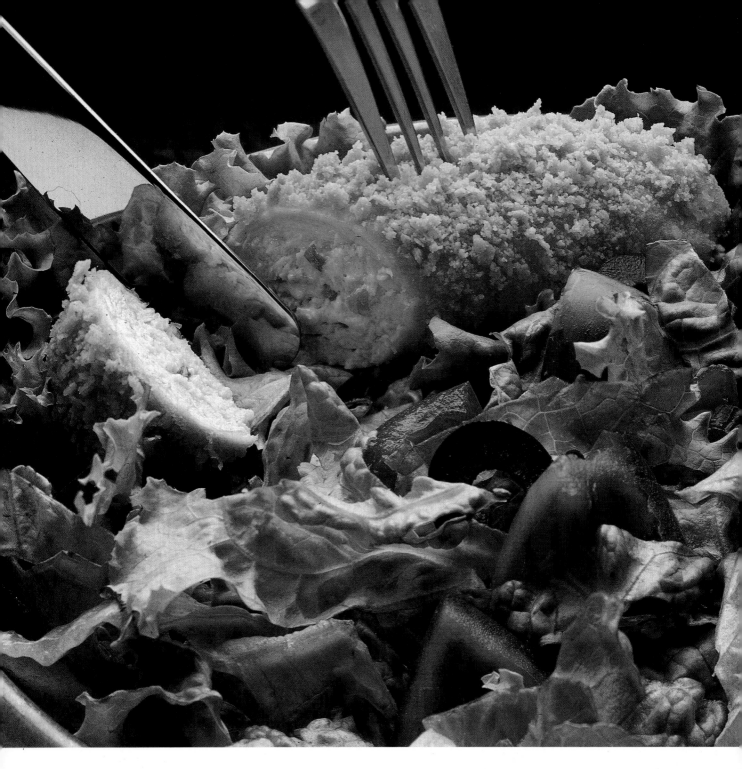

Chicken Viejo

Serve on lettuce with chopped tomatoes, sliced black olives and taco sauce.

Patricia Johnson
Mission Viejo, California

2 boneless whole chicken
   breasts (10 to 12 oz. each)
   skin removed, cut in half
¼ cup butter or margarine,
   divided

2 tablespoons sharp
   pasteurized process cheese
   spread
1 tablespoon sliced green
   onion

1 tablespoon canned chopped
   green chilies, drained
½ teaspoon salt
1 cup Cheddar cheese
   crackers
2 teaspoons Mexican
   seasoning, optional

4 servings

How to Microwave Chicken Viejo

Pound each chicken breast half between two sheets of plastic wrap to ¼-inch thickness. Set aside. Place 2 tablespoons butter in small bowl. Microwave at 30% (Medium Low) for 15 to 30 seconds, or until softened.

Stir in cheese spread, onion, chilies and salt. Spread one-fourth of cheese mixture at one end of each chicken breast half.

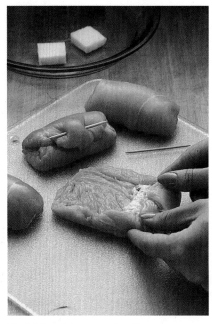

Fold in sides and roll up, enclosing filling. Secure with wooden picks. Set aside. Place remaining 2 tablespoons butter in 9-inch pie plate. Microwave at High for 45 seconds to 1 minute, or until butter melts. Set aside.

Place crackers in food processor or blender bowl. Process until fine crumbs. Place crumbs in shallow dish. Stir in Mexican seasoning.

Dip each stuffed breast in melted butter, then in crumbs to coat, pressing lightly.

Place seam-side down on roasting rack. Microwave at 70% (Medium High) for 8 to 10 minutes, or until chicken is firm and no longer pink, rotating rack 2 or 3 times. Remove wooden picks.

Stuffed Chicken Rolls

Donna M. Wright
Orlando, Florida

2 boneless whole chicken breasts (10 to 12 oz. each) skin removed, cut in half
⅓ cup ricotta cheese
2 tablespoons grated Parmesan cheese
1 tablespoon sliced green onion
¼ teaspoon dried basil leaves
¼ teaspoon dried oregano leaves
⅛ teaspoon dried thyme leaves
⅛ teaspoon salt
⅛ teaspoon pepper
1 jar (15½ oz.) extra-thick spaghetti sauce
1 cup shredded mozzarella cheese

4 servings

Pound each chicken breast half between two sheets of plastic wrap to ¼-inch thickness. Set aside. In small mixing bowl, combine ricotta and Parmesan cheeses, onion, basil, oregano, thyme, salt and pepper. Mix well. Spread one-fourth of cheese mixture down center of each chicken breast half. Fold in sides and roll up, enclosing filling. Secure with wooden picks. Arrange stuffed rolls seam-side down in 9-inch square baking dish. Pour spaghetti sauce over chicken. Cover with wax paper. Micro-wave at High for 11 to 15 minutes, or until chicken is firm and no longer pink, rotating dish twice. Remove wooden picks. Top with mozzarella cheese. Reduce power to 50% (Medium). Microwave for 2 to 4 minutes, or until cheese melts. Serve with hot cooked pasta.

Quick Chicken Dinner

Ruth Ann Davis
Lost Creek, West Virginia

¼ cup butter or margarine
⅔ cup herb seasoned stuffing mix
2 teaspoons dried parsley flakes
1 pkg. (10 oz.) frozen chopped broccoli
2 cups sliced fresh mushrooms
1 pkg. (4.6 oz.) chicken-flavored rice and sauce mix
1 tablespoon finely chopped onion
1¾ cups water
1½ to 2 cups cut-up cooked chicken

4 to 6 servings

Place butter in small mixing bowl. Microwave at High for 1¼ to 1½ minutes, or until butter melts. Stir in stuffing mix and parsley. Mix well. Set aside.

Unwrap broccoli and place on plate. Microwave at High for 2½ to 3 minutes, or until defrosted. Drain. Set aside. In 2-quart casserole, combine mushrooms, rice and sauce mix, onion and water. Mix well. Cover. Microwave at High for 10 to 12 minutes, or until rice is tender, stirring once. Stir in broccoli and chicken. Top with stuffing mixture. Microwave at High for 7 to 9 minutes, or until heated through, rotating casserole once.

Creamy Quick Chicken Dinner: Follow recipe above, adding 1 can (10¾ oz.) condensed cream of mushroom soup with broccoli and chicken.

Golden Chicken Nuggets

Joyce A. Kopsack
Pittsford, Vermont

- 2 tablespoons butter or margarine
- ½ cup chopped onion
- 3 tablespoons all-purpose flour
- 1 tablespoon curry powder
- 1 teaspoon dried parsley flakes
- ¾ teaspoon salt
- ¼ teaspoon paprika
- ⅛ teaspoon pepper
- 1 cup ready-to-serve chicken broth
- ¾ cup orange marmalade
- 2 cups sliced fresh mushrooms
- 3 boneless whole chicken breasts (10 to 12 oz. each) skin removed, cut into 1½-inch pieces

4 to 6 servings

In 1-quart casserole, combine butter and onion. Microwave at High for 2 to 3 minutes, or until onion is tender. Stir in flour, curry powder, parsley, salt, paprika and pepper. Blend in broth. Microwave at High for 3 to 5 minutes, or until mixture thickens and bubbles, stirring twice. Stir in marmalade until melted. Stir in mushrooms. Cover. Set aside. Place chicken in 2-quart casserole. Cover with wax paper. Microwave at High for 7 to 9 minutes, or until chicken is no longer pink, stirring twice. Drain. Stir mushroom sauce into chicken. Microwave, uncovered, at High for 2 to 3 minutes, or until mushrooms are tender. Serve over hot cooked rice.

Quick Sweet & Sour Chicken ▲

Laurie Burns
Plymouth, Minnesota

- 1 can (15¼ oz.) pineapple chunks in juice
- 2 tablespoons cornstarch
- ½ cup dark corn syrup
- ¼ cup vinegar
- 2 tablespoons soy sauce
- 2 tablespoons catsup
- 1 clove garlic, minced
- 2 boneless whole chicken breasts (10 to 12 oz. each) skin removed, cut into 1-inch pieces
- ½ medium green pepper, cut into ½-inch pieces
- 2 green onions, sliced ¼ inch thick

4 to 6 servings

Drain pineapple juice into 2-quart casserole. Reserve pineapple chunks. Blend cornstarch and pineapple juice. Stir in corn syrup, vinegar, soy sauce, catsup and garlic. Stir in chicken. Cover. Microwave at High for 9 to 15 minutes, or until sauce is thickened and translucent and chicken is no longer pink, stirring twice. Mix in pineapple chunks, green pepper and onions. Microwave at High for 2 to 4 minutes, or until heated through, stirring once. Serve over hot cooked rice.

Turkey Tetrazzini

Susie Shupe
Indianola, Iowa

Serve with favorite tossed salad or romaine leaves topped with oil and vinegar dressing.

- 1 lb. uncooked spaghetti
- 1 tablespoon butter or margarine
- 1 pkg. (2½ oz.) slivered almonds
- ⅓ cup chopped green pepper
- 1 medium onion, chopped
- 12 oz. pasteurized process cheese spread, cut into ¾-inch cubes
- 1 can (10¾ oz.) condensed cream of mushroom soup
- ⅓ cup milk
- 1 can (4 oz.) sliced mushrooms, drained
- 3 cups cut-up cooked turkey, ¾-inch cubes

8 to 10 servings

Prepare spaghetti as directed on package. Rinse and drain. Set aside. In 9-inch pie plate, combine butter and almonds. Microwave at High for 4 to 6 minutes, or until light golden brown, stirring after every 2 minutes. Set aside. In 3-quart casserole, combine green pepper and onion. Cover. Microwave at High for 3 to 4 minutes, or until tender, stirring once. Stir in cheese, soup, milk and mushrooms. Microwave, uncovered, at High for 3 to 6 minutes, or until cheese melts, stirring twice. Stir in turkey and spaghetti to coat with sauce. Cover. Microwave at High for 6 to 9 minutes, or until heated through, stirring once. Top with toasted almonds.

Oriental Almond Turkey

Ernestine Keane
Cypress, California

Perfect for the late-night evening meal.

8 turkey cutlets (2 to 3 oz.
   each) ¼ inch thick
¼ cup soy sauce
¼ teaspoon garlic powder
⅛ teaspoon pepper
3 tablespoons butter or
   margarine, divided
⅓ cup slivered almonds
1 medium onion, thinly sliced
½ cup chopped green pepper
½ cup sliced fresh mushrooms
½ cup dry vermouth

4 to 6 servings

How to Microwave Oriental Almond Turkey

Place turkey cutlets in large plastic food storage bag. In 1-cup measure, mix soy sauce, garlic powder and pepper. Pour over cutlets. Secure bag.

Marinate for 15 to 20 minutes on counter. Meanwhile, in 9-inch pie plate, combine 1 tablespoon butter and almonds. Microwave at High for 4 to 6 minutes, or until light golden brown, stirring after every 2 minutes. Set aside.

Combine remaining 2 tablespoons butter, onion, green pepper and mushrooms in 10-inch square casserole. Cover. Microwave at High for 3 to 4 minutes, or until onion is tender-crisp, stirring once.

Lift cutlets from marinade. Arrange in 10-inch square casserole, spooning vegetables over cutlets.

Pour vermouth over cutlets and vegetables. Reduce power to 70% (Medium High). Microwave for 7 to 12 minutes, or until turkey is firm and no longer pink, rearranging cutlets once. Let stand, covered, for 3 minutes.

Top with toasted almonds. Serve over hot cooked rice.

Seafood

◀ Oriental Shrimp

Karen L. Braucher
Mohrsville, Pennsylvania

1 tablespoon vegetable oil
1 tablespoon butter or
   margarine
1 medium red pepper, cut into
   ½-inch strips
1 cup diagonally sliced carrots,
   ⅛ inch thick
1 cup diagonally sliced celery,
   ⅛ inch thick
½ cup fresh broccoli flowerets
½ cup fresh cauliflowerets

Sauce:
⅔ cup ready-to-serve chicken
   broth
3 tablespoons soy sauce
1 tablespoon cornstarch
¼ teaspoon sugar
¼ teaspoon ground ginger
   Dash dried crushed red
   pepper

1 lb. medium shrimp, shelled
   and deveined
1 cup sliced fresh mushrooms
¼ cup sliced green onions

4 to 6 servings

In 2-quart casserole, combine
oil, butter, red pepper, carrots,
celery, broccoli and cauliflower.
Cover. Microwave at High for 5
to 9 minutes, or just until vegetables are tender-crisp, stirring
once or twice. Set aside.

In 2-cup measure, blend broth,
soy sauce and cornstarch. Stir
in sugar, ginger and dried red
pepper. Microwave at High for
2½ to 4½ minutes, or until
mixture is thickened and translucent, stirring twice. Pour over
vegetables. Stir in shrimp, mushrooms and onions. Re-cover.
Microwave at High for 4 to 5½
minutes, or until shrimp are
opaque, stirring once or twice.
Let stand, covered, for 1 minute.
Serve over hot cooked rice.

Fish Creole ▲

Donald D. Long
Denver, Colorado

1 cup hot water
1 can (8 oz.) tomato sauce
½ cup chopped onion
⅓ cup uncooked long grain
   white rice
½ teaspoon dried basil leaves

¼ teaspoon dried tarragon
   leaves
¼ teaspoon salt
¼ teaspoon hot pepper sauce
12 oz. cod fillets, about ¾ inch
   thick, cut into ¾-inch cubes

4 servings

In 1½-quart casserole, combine all ingredients, except cod. Mix
well. Cover. Microwave at High for 5 minutes. Reduce power to
50% (Medium). Microwave for 20 to 26 minutes, or until rice is
tender. Stir in cod. Re-cover. Microwave at 50% (Medium) for 4 to 5
minutes, or until fish flakes easily with fork, stirring once. Let stand,
covered, for 3 minutes.

Crab-stuffed Fillet of Sole

Camilla Chappell
Portsmouth, Rhode Island

2 teaspoons butter or
   margarine
¼ cup sliced almonds

Stuffing:

1 tablespoon butter or
   margarine
⅓ cup finely chopped celery
¼ cup finely chopped onion
1 can (6 oz.) crab meat,
   rinsed, drained and
   cartilage removed
2 tablespoons seasoned dry
   bread crumbs
1 tablespoon sherry

4 sole fillets, about ¼ inch
   thick, 10 to 12 inches long

Sauce:

1 can (10¾ oz.) condensed
   cream of shrimp soup
2 tablespoons snipped fresh
   parsley
1 tablespoon sherry
1 tablespoon lemon juice
   Paprika

4 servings

How to Microwave Crab-stuffed Fillet of Sole

Combine butter and almonds in 9-inch pie plate. Microwave at High for 4 to 6 minutes, or until light golden brown, stirring after every 2 minutes. Set aside.

Combine 1 tablespoon butter, celery and onion in small mixing bowl for stuffing. Cover with plastic wrap. Microwave at High for 2 to 3 minutes, or until vegetables are tender.

Stir in remaining stuffing ingredients. Mix well. Spread one-fourth of stuffing down center of each fillet.

Roll up, enclosing stuffing. Arrange crab-stuffed sole, seam-side down in 9-inch square baking dish.

Blend sauce ingredients, except paprika, in small mixing bowl. Pour evenly over stuffed sole. Sprinkle with paprika. Cover with plastic wrap.

Microwave at High for 10 to 13 minutes, or until center of fish roll flakes easily with fork, rotating dish once or twice. Let stand, covered, for 3 minutes. Top with toasted almonds.

◀ Spinach & Crab Linguine

Inge McElrath
Lake Ronkonkoma, New York

1 pkg. (10 oz.) frozen
   chopped spinach
2 tablespoons butter or
   margarine
1½ cups sliced fresh
   mushrooms
1 shallot, chopped
2 cans (6 oz. each) crab
   meat, rinsed, drained and
   cartilage removed
1 can (10¾ oz.) condensed
   cream of shrimp soup
⅓ cup dry white wine
⅔ cup whipping cream or
   half-and-half
1 pkg. (7 oz.) linguine

4 to 6 servings

Unwrap spinach and place on plate. Microwave at High for 4½ to 6 minutes, or until warm. Drain thoroughly, pressing to remove excess moisture. Set aside. In 1½-quart casserole, combine butter, mushrooms and shallot. Cover. Microwave at High for 2 to 4 minutes, or until shallot is tender, stirring once. Stir in crab meat, soup, wine and spinach. Blend in whipping cream. Re-cover. Reduce power to 70% (Medium High). Microwave for 8 to 10 minutes, or until heated through, stirring 2 or 3 times. Meanwhile, prepare linguine as directed on package. Rinse and drain. Serve sauce over hot linguine.

Easy Fish & Capers

This quick and delicious recipe fits well in a busy schedule.

Mar-Sue Ratzke
Cypress, California

1 lb. orange roughy or
   haddock fillets, ½ to ¾ inch
   thick, cut into serving-size
   pieces
¼ cup butter or margarine
2 tablespoons capers, drained
2 tablespoons grated
   Parmesan cheese
   Paprika

4 servings

Arrange orange roughy pieces in 10-inch square casserole. Place butter in 1-cup measure. Microwave at High for 1¼ to 1½ minutes, or until butter melts. Pour evenly over orange roughy. Top with capers. Microwave, uncovered, at High for 3 minutes. Rearrange pieces. Top with cheese. Sprinkle with paprika. Microwave at High for 2 to 6 minutes, or until fish flakes easily with fork.

Jean's Fish Fillets

Jean Gallina
East Amherst, New York

- 2 tablespoons butter or margarine
- 12 oz. flounder fillets, about ¼ inch thick, cut into serving-size pieces
- ¼ teaspoon salt
  Pepper
- 2 tablespoons finely chopped onion
- 2 tablespoons snipped fresh parsley
- 1 medium tomato, seeded and chopped
- ¼ teaspoon dried basil leaves, optional
- ¼ cup shredded Cheddar cheese
- ¼ cup shredded Swiss cheese

4 servings

Place butter in 10-inch square casserole. Microwave at High for 45 seconds to 1 minute, or until butter melts. Add flounder, turning to coat both sides. Arrange flounder with thickest portions toward outside of casserole. Sprinkle with salt, pepper, onion, parsley, tomato and basil. Cover. Reduce power to 70% (Medium High). Microwave for 9 to 13 minutes, or until fish in center flakes easily with fork, rotating casserole once or twice.

Top with Cheddar and Swiss cheeses. Re-cover. Microwave at High for 45 seconds to 1 minute, or until cheese melts. Let stand, covered, for 2 minutes.

Seafood-Vegetable Medley

Mrs. Lynn M. Sewell
Elwood, New Jersey

- 2 tablespoons butter or margarine
- 1 medium onion, thinly sliced
- 1 tablespoon snipped fresh parsley
- ¼ teaspoon dried tarragon leaves
- 1½ cups thinly sliced zucchini or summer squash
- 1 medium tomato, cut into 1½-inch pieces
- 12 fresh mushrooms, cut in half
- 4 seafood sticks (1 oz. each) cut into 1-inch pieces
- ¼ lb. bay scallops
- Salt
- Pepper
- 4 oz. sliced Monterey Jack cheese, ⅛ inch thick

4 servings

How to Microwave Seafood-Vegetable Medley

Combine butter, onion, parsley and tarragon in 1½-quart casserole. Cover. Microwave at High for 3 minutes.

Stir in zucchini, tomato and mushrooms. Re-cover. Microwave at High for 4 to 5 minutes, or until zucchini is tender-crisp, stirring once.

Stir in seafood pieces and scallops. Re-cover. Microwave at High for 2½ to 3½ minutes, or until scallops are opaque, stirring once.

Lift vegetables and seafood with slotted spoon and divide among four individual (12 to 15 oz. each) casseroles. Sprinkle each with salt and pepper.

Arrange cheese slices over seafood mixture.

Place under preheated broiler 3 to 4 inches from heat, until cheese melts, 2 to 3 minutes. Serve with toasted French bread.

Shrimp & Scallop Stir-fry

Kathy Smith
Suitland, Maryland

Kathy's family prefers this delicious main dish served over brown rice.

2 cups frozen Japanese-style vegetables
1 pkg. (6 oz.) frozen pea pods
⅓ cup water
1 tablespoon cornstarch
3 tablespoons soy sauce
3 tablespoons sherry
1 tablespoon vegetable oil
2 teaspoons sugar
½ teaspoon ground ginger
1 lb. medium shrimp, shelled and deveined
½ lb. bay scallops

6 servings

In 2-quart casserole, combine Japanese-style vegetables and pea pods. Cover. Microwave at High for 4 to 5 minutes, or until vegetables are defrosted, stirring after half the time to break apart. Let stand, covered, for 5 minutes. Drain. Set aside.

In 2-cup measure, blend water, cornstarch, soy sauce, sherry, oil, sugar and ginger. Microwave at High for 3 to 4 minutes, or until mixture is thickened and translucent, stirring twice. Pour over vegetables. Stir in shrimp and scallops. Re-cover. Microwave at High for 7 to 10 minutes, or until shrimp and scallops are opaque, stirring twice. Let stand, covered, for 3 minutes. Serve over hot cooked brown or white rice.

Scampi

Harold R. Ferguson
Walnut Creek, California

Butter mixture can be spread on French bread and toasted under the broiler.

¼ cup butter or margarine
¾ cup olive oil
¼ cup snipped fresh parsley
2 tablespoons fresh lemon
   juice
2 cloves garlic, minced
½ teaspoon salt
½ teaspoon pepper
1½ lbs. medium shrimp,
   shelled and deveined

4 to 6 servings

Place butter in 10-inch square casserole. Microwave at High for 1¼ to 1½ minutes, or until butter melts. Blend in olive oil. Stir in parsley, lemon juice, garlic, salt and pepper. Add shrimp, stirring to coat with butter mixture. Cover. Reduce power to 70% (Medium High). Microwave for 6 to 9 minutes, or until shrimp are opaque, stirring twice. Let stand, covered, for 2 to 3 minutes. Place shrimp on platter or serve over hot cooked rice. Serve with butter mixture as a sauce.

Sole with Mustard Sauce

Jill Dix Ghnassia
New Hartford, Connecticut

¼ cup butter or margarine,
   divided
2 shallots, thinly sliced
1 lb. sole fillets, ¼ to ½ inch
   thick, cut into serving-size
   pieces
1 cup sliced fresh mushrooms
½ cup white wine
1 tablespoon lemon juice
2 teaspoons snipped fresh
   parsley
2 teaspoons Dijon mustard
¼ teaspoon salt
⅛ teaspoon pepper
2 tablespoons all-purpose flour

4 servings

How to Microwave Sole with Mustard Sauce

Combine 2 tablespoons butter and shallots in small bowl. Microwave at High for 1 to 2 minutes, or until shallots are tender-crisp.

Arrange sole in 10-inch square casserole with thickest portions toward outside of casserole. Pour shallots and butter mixture over sole. Top with mushrooms.

Mix wine, lemon juice, parsley, Dijon mustard, salt and pepper in 1-cup measure. Pour over sole and vegetables. Cover. Microwave at High for 7 to 9 minutes, or until fish flakes easily with fork, rotating casserole once or twice.

Place sole and vegetables on platter. Set aside. Pour cooking liquid into 1-cup measure. Add water to equal 1 cup. Set aside.

Place remaining 2 tablespoons butter in 2-cup measure. Microwave at High for 45 seconds to 1 minute, or until butter melts.

Stir in flour. Blend in cooking liquid. Microwave at High for 1¼ to 1¾ minutes, or until mixture thickens and bubbles, stirring once. Pour sauce over sole before serving.

Shrimp & Creamy Noodles

Mrs. Pearl Lakey
Seymour, Missouri

- 3 cups uncooked egg noodles
- 3 tablespoons butter or margarine
- ¼ cup chopped onion
- 2 tablespoons all-purpose flour
- 1 teaspoon dried parsley flakes
- ½ teaspoon dried dill weed
- ¼ teaspoon salt
- ¼ teaspoon dried tarragon leaves
- 1⅓ cups milk
- ½ cup dairy sour cream
- ⅓ cup grated Parmesan cheese
- 2 cans (4¼ oz. each) small shrimp, rinsed and drained
- ⅔ cup canned French fried onions

4 to 6 servings

Prepare noodles as directed on package. Rinse and drain. Set aside. In 1½-quart casserole, combine butter and onion. Cover. Microwave at High for 1½ to 2½ minutes, or until onion is tender. Stir in flour, parsley, dill weed, salt and tarragon. Blend in milk. Microwave at High for 3½ to 5 minutes, or until mixture thickens and bubbles, stirring twice. Stir in sour cream, cheese, shrimp and noodles. Re-cover. Reduce power to 70% (Medium High). Microwave for 6 to 8 minutes, or until heated through, stirring once. During last 2 to 3 minutes of cooking time, uncover casserole and sprinkle with onions.

Seasoned Coated Fish ▲

Kandace A. Beale
Kersey, Pennsylvania

- ¼ cup butter or margarine
- ⅔ cup unseasoned dry bread crumbs
- ¼ cup grated Parmesan cheese
- ½ teaspoon dried basil leaves
- ¼ teaspoon garlic salt
- 1 lb. haddock fillets, ½ to ¾ inch thick, cut into serving-size pieces
- Dried parsley flakes (optional)

4 servings

Place butter in 9-inch square baking dish. Microwave at High for 1¼ to 1½ minutes, or until butter melts. Set aside. On sheet of wax paper, combine bread crumbs, cheese, basil and garlic salt. Dip haddock in melted butter, then roll in crumbs to coat both sides, pressing lightly. Arrange haddock pieces on roasting rack with thickest portions toward outside of rack. Microwave, uncovered, at High for 6 to 9 minutes, or until fish flakes easily with fork, rotating rack once. Garnish with parsley.

Haya's Shrimp ▶

Barb Gray
Ballwin, Missouri

- 1 tablespoon all-purpose flour
- ¼ cup vegetable oil
- ¾ cup red wine
- 2 tablespoons lemon juice
- 2 tablespoons tomato paste
- 2 tablespoons teriyaki sauce
- ⅛ teaspoon paprika
  Dash to ⅛ teaspoon
  cayenne
- 1 clove garlic, minced
- 1 lb. medium shrimp, shelled
  and deveined

4 servings

In 1½-quart casserole, blend
flour and oil. Stir in remaining
ingredients, except shrimp.
Microwave, uncovered, at High
for 3 to 4 minutes, or until
mixture thickens and bubbles,
stirring once. Stir in shrimp.
Cover. Reduce power to 50%
(Medium). Microwave for 4 to
7 minutes, or until shrimp are
opaque, stirring twice. Let stand,
covered, for 3 to 5 minutes.
Serve over hot cooked rice.

Tuna-Potato Pie

Mrs. Arlene Pepin
North Branford, Connecticut

- ½ cup chopped green pepper
- 2 tablespoons sliced green
  onion
- 1 pkg. (14 oz.) frozen cottage
  fries
- 1 can (6½ oz.) tuna, drained
- 1 can (4 oz.) sliced
  mushrooms, drained
- 1 can (10¾ oz.) condensed
  cream of celery soup
- ¼ cup milk
- 2 teaspoons lemon juice
- ½ teaspoon dried dill weed
- ⅛ teaspoon pepper

4 to 6 servings

In small mixing bowl, combine green pepper and onion. Cover
with plastic wrap. Microwave at High for 1½ to 2½ minutes, or until
green pepper is tender-crisp. Set aside. Arrange cottage fries over
bottom and along sides of 9-inch round baking dish. Cover with
plastic wrap. Microwave at High for 5 to 7 minutes, or until heated
through, rotating dish once. Layer tuna, mushrooms and green
pepper mixture over potatoes. In small mixing bowl, blend soup,
milk, lemon juice, dill weed and pepper. Spoon evenly over tuna
and vegetables. Cover with plastic wrap. Microwave at High for 6
to 8 minutes, or until heated through, rotating dish once. Let stand,
covered, for 3 minutes.

Eggs & Cheese

◄ Broccoli-Rice Cheese Pie

Lucy L. Archer
Orange Park, Florida

Filling:

1 pkg. (10 oz.) frozen chopped broccoli
¾ cup shredded Cheddar cheese
1 jar (4½ oz.) sliced mushrooms, drained
2 eggs, beaten
1 tablespoon all-purpose flour
½ teaspoon salt

Crust:

1½ cups hot cooked rice
¾ cup shredded Cheddar cheese
1 egg, beaten
Paprika, optional

4 to 6 servings

Unwrap broccoli and place in 1-quart casserole. Microwave at High for 4 to 5 minutes, or until defrosted, stirring after half the time to break apart. Drain. In medium mixing bowl, combine all filling ingredients. Mix well. Set aside. In small mixing bowl, combine rice, cheese and egg. Mix well. Spread over bottom and sides of 9-inch pie plate. Spoon filling into crust. Cover with wax paper. Microwave at 70% (Medium High) for 9½ to 13 minutes, or until center of filling is set. Let stand, covered, for 5 minutes. Sprinkle with paprika. Cut into wedges.

Italian Scramble

Ellen Lavin Lickhalter
Carlsbad, California

¼ lb. Italian sausage
6 eggs
3 tablespoons whipping cream
2 tablespoons grated Parmesan cheese
2 tablespoons snipped fresh parsley
½ teaspoon lemon juice
¼ teaspoon dried basil leaves
¼ teaspoon salt
⅛ teaspoon pepper
4 oz. mozzarella cheese, cut into ½-inch cubes
½ cup sliced fresh mushrooms
2 tablespoons sliced pimiento-stuffed or black olives

4 to 6 servings

Crumble sausage into 1½-quart casserole. Cover with wax paper. Microwave at High for 2 to 2½ minutes, or until sausage is no longer pink, stirring once to break apart. Drain. Set aside. In medium mixing bowl, combine eggs, whipping cream, Parmesan cheese, parsley, lemon juice, basil, salt and pepper. Beat well. Stir in mozzarella cheese, mushrooms and olives. Pour over sausage. Microwave, uncovered, at High for 6 to 8 minutes, or just until eggs are set, stirring after every 2 minutes. Let stand, covered with wax paper, for 2 minutes.

Betty's Brunch Deluxe

Clara C. Carli
North Arlington, New Jersey

1 pkg. (12 oz.) frozen hash
   brown potatoes
6 eggs
⅓ cup whipping cream
1 cup shredded Cheddar
   cheese
1 cup cubed fully cooked ham
   or Canadian bacon,
   ¼-inch cubes
2 teaspoons freeze-dried
   chives
¼ teaspoon salt
⅛ teaspoon pepper

4 to 6 servings

Place potatoes in 9-inch square baking dish. Cover with plastic wrap. Microwave at High for 5 to 7 minutes, or until potatoes are hot, stirring after every 2 minutes to break apart. Set aside. In medium mixing bowl, blend eggs and whipping cream. Stir in cheese, ham, chives, salt and pepper. Pour over potatoes. Mix well. Cover with wax paper. Reduce power to 50% (Medium). Microwave for 17 to 28 minutes, or until egg mixture is set, stirring after every 5 minutes.

Mushroom Tetrazzini ▶

Patricia R. Harrah
Akron, Ohio

1 pkg. (7 oz.) spaghetti
¼ cup butter or margarine
1 cup sliced fresh
 mushrooms
½ cup chopped onion
¼ cup all-purpose flour
2 tablespoons sherry
½ teaspoon salt
⅛ teaspoon pepper
1½ cups milk
4 oz. Provolone cheese, cut
 into ¼-inch cubes
4 oz. mozzarella cheese, cut
 into ¼-inch cubes
2 tablespoons snipped fresh
 parsley

4 to 6 servings

Prepare spaghetti as directed on package. Rinse and drain. Cover. Set aside. In 2-quart casserole, combine butter, mushrooms and onion. Microwave at High for 4 to 6 minutes, or until mushrooms are tender, stirring once. Stir in flour, sherry, salt and pepper. Blend in milk. Microwave at High for 4 to 6 minutes, or until mixture thickens and bubbles, stirring after every 2 minutes. Stir in Provolone and mozzarella cheeses. Microwave at High for 1½ to 2 minutes, or until mixture can be stirred smooth, stirring after every minute. Pour cheese mixture over spaghetti. Toss to coat. Microwave at High for 1 to 2 minutes, or until heated through. Sprinkle with parsley.

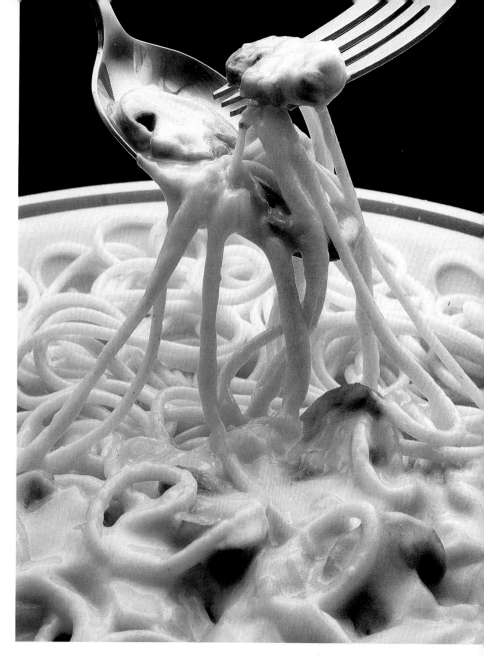

Green Noodles Carbonara

Sandy Kennedy
Chicago, Illinois

4 slices bacon
4 cups uncooked spinach
 egg noodles
¼ cup butter or margarine
½ cup grated Parmesan
 cheese

2 eggs, beaten
½ cup whipping cream
¼ teaspoon freshly ground
 pepper

4 servings

Place bacon on paper towel-lined plate. Cover with another paper towel. Microwave at High for 3½ to 5½ minutes, or until crisp. Cool slightly. Crumble. Set aside. Prepare noodles as directed on package. Rinse and drain. Cover. Set aside. Place butter in 2-quart casserole. Microwave at 30% (Medium Low) for 15 to 45 seconds, or until softened, checking after every 15 seconds. Stir in cheese. Stir in bacon, eggs, whipping cream and pepper. Add noodles. Toss to coat. Microwave at 50% (Medium) for 4 to 6 minutes, or until heated through, stirring after every 2 minutes.

Chiles Rellenos José

Donald K. LaBerenz
Denver, Colorado

- 1 can (7 oz.) whole green chilies, drained
- 3 oz. Monterey Jack cheese, thinly sliced
- 1 cup shredded Cheddar cheese
- ½ teaspoon paprika
- 1¼ cups milk
- ¼ cup all-purpose flour
- 5 eggs
- ½ teaspoon salt
- ¼ teaspoon hot pepper sauce
- ⅛ teaspoon pepper

Salsa:

- 2 medium tomatoes, seeded and coarsely chopped
- 1 small onion, cut into 4 pieces
- 3 tablespoons canned diced green chilies, drained
- 4 teaspoons vinegar
- 1 tablespoon finely chopped fresh cilantro leaves
- 1 teaspoon salt

6 servings

How to Microwave Chiles Rellenos José

Place chilies on paper towels. Cut lengthwise slit in each chili. Remove seeds. Cut Monterey Jack cheese to fit inside each green chili.

Arrange stuffed chilies in 9-inch round baking dish. Top with Cheddar cheese. Sprinkle with paprika. Set aside. In 4-cup measure, blend milk and flour.

Mix in eggs, salt, hot pepper sauce and pepper. Beat well. Microwave at High for 3 to 5 minutes, or until mixture is hot and begins to set around edges, beating with whisk after every minute. Pour over stuffed chilies. Cover with plastic wrap.

Place dish on saucer in microwave oven. Microwave at 50% (Medium) for 15 to 22 minutes, or until no uncooked egg mixture remains on the bottom, rotating dish twice. Let stand, covered, for 6 to 8 minutes.

Combine all Salsa ingredients in food processor or blender bowl. Process until almost smooth.

Cut Chiles Rellenos into wedges. Top with Salsa. Refrigerate any extra Salsa and use as a dip for tortilla chips.

Mexican Seasoned Potatoes

Vegetable Side Dishes

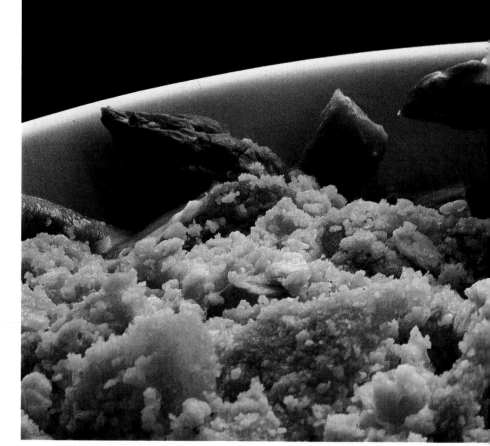

Cheesy Bacon Asparagus

Mrs. Merrill Stateler
McComb, Ohio

2 pkgs. (10 oz. each) frozen
    asparagus cuts
2 slices bacon, cut up
2 cups Cheddar cheese
    crackers, finely crushed,
    divided
1 can (10¾ oz.) condensed
    cream of mushroom soup
2 tablespoons milk
1 tablespoon lemon juice
⅛ teaspoon pepper

6 to 8 servings

How to Microwave Cheesy Bacon Asparagus

Unwrap asparagus and place in 1½-quart casserole. Microwave at High for 5 to 6 minutes, or until defrosted, stirring once to break apart. Drain. Set aside.

Place bacon in small mixing bowl. Microwave at High for 2 to 3 minutes, or until brown and crisp, stirring once.

Stir ½ cup crushed crackers into bacon and fat. Set aside. Sprinkle remaining crushed crackers over asparagus.

Combine soup, milk, lemon juice and pepper in small mixing bowl until well blended.

Spoon evenly over asparagus. Cover. Microwave at High for 8 to 10 minutes, or until heated through, stirring once.

Sprinkle asparagus with bacon and crushed crackers. Microwave, uncovered, at High for 2 minutes.

◄ Spiced Oriental-style Carrots

Kaye Dunn
Van Buren, Arkansas

Can be served hot or cold.

3 cups sliced carrots, ¼ inch
   thick
½ cup chopped green pepper
¼ cup finely chopped onion
3 tablespoons water
1 can (8 oz.) sliced water
   chestnuts, drained
1 can (7¾ oz.) semi-
   condensed tomato soup
½ cup sugar
2 teaspoons vinegar
1 teaspoon soy sauce
½ teaspoon salt
½ teaspoon prepared mustard
⅛ teaspoon pepper

6 to 8 servings

In 1½-quart casserole, combine
carrots, green pepper, onion and
water. Cover. Microwave at High
for 8 to 10 minutes, or until carrots are tender-crisp, stirring
once. Stir in remaining ingredients. Re-cover. Microwave at
High for 3 to 4 minutes, or until
heated through.

Broccoli Casserole ▲

Joelle A. Faulks
Earlville, New York

1 pkg. (16 oz.) frozen broccoli
   cuts
1½ cups cheese and garlic
   croutons
1 can (10¾ oz.) condensed
   cream of mushroom soup
½ cup shredded Swiss
   cheese
½ cup shredded Cheddar
   cheese
¼ cup milk

6 to 8 servings

Place broccoli in 2-quart casserole. Cover. Microwave at High
for 3 to 4 minutes, or until
defrosted, stirring once to break
apart. Drain. Stir in croutons,
soup, cheeses and milk. Mix
well. Re-cover. Microwave at
High for 8 to 11 minutes, or until
heated through, stirring twice.
Let stand, covered, for 3
minutes before serving.

Baked Cabbage

Sharon Borron
Jefferson City, Missouri

1 medium head cabbage,
   shredded, about 8 cups
1 can (10¾ oz.) condensed
   cream of celery soup
⅔ cup milk
½ teaspoon caraway seed,
   crushed
½ teaspoon salt
¼ teaspoon pepper
⅓ cup finely shredded
   pasteurized process
   American cheese

4 to 6 servings

Place cabbage in 2-quart
casserole. In small mixing bowl,
blend soup, milk, caraway, salt
and pepper. Pour over cabbage.
Mix well. Cover. Microwave at
High for 12 to 16 minutes, or
until cabbage is tender-crisp,
stirring once. Sprinkle with
cheese. Re-cover. Microwave
at High for 30 seconds to
1 minute, or until cheese melts.

Cheesy Cauliflower ▲

Opal Schubert
Princeton, Illinois

1 medium head cauliflower, about 2 lbs., trimmed
1 cup shredded Cheddar cheese
½ cup mayonnaise
1 tablespoon prepared horseradish mustard

4 to 6 servings

Place cauliflower stem-side down on serving plate. Cover with plastic wrap. Microwave at High for 7 to 11 minutes, or until tender, rotating plate twice. Set aside. In small mixing bowl, combine cheese, mayonnaise and horseradish mustard. Mix well. Unwrap cauliflower. Spread cheese mixture evenly over cauliflower. Microwave at High for 1½ to 3 minutes, or just until cheese begins to melt. Let stand for 3 minutes.

Scalloped Corn

Cynthia R. Timmel
Vancouver, Washington

2 tablespoons butter or margarine
½ cup chopped celery
¼ cup chopped onion
¼ cup chopped green pepper
1 can (16 oz.) cream-style corn
1 cup shredded sharp Cheddar cheese
1 cup milk
½ cup saltine cracker crumbs
½ cup quick-cooking rolled oats
2 eggs, beaten
¾ teaspoon salt
Paprika

6 to 8 servings

In 1½-quart casserole, combine butter, celery, onion and green pepper. Cover. Microwave at High for 3 to 4 minutes, or until vegetables are tender-crisp, stirring once. Stir in corn, cheese, milk, cracker crumbs, oats, eggs and salt. Mix well. Reduce power to 70% (Medium High). Microwave, uncovered, for 15 to 20 minutes, or until mixture thickens and appears set, stirring after every 5 minutes. Sprinkle with paprika.

Horseradish Creamed ▲ Potatoes

Maurine Miller Welch
Spring Hill, Florida

2 tablespoons prepared horseradish
1 tablespoon instant chicken bouillon granules
2 teaspoons all-purpose flour
¼ teaspoon salt
⅛ teaspoon pepper
1 cup half-and-half
3½ cups peeled cubed potatoes, ¾-inch cubes
Snipped fresh parsley or watercress (optional)

4 to 6 servings

In 1½-quart casserole, combine horseradish, bouillon, flour, salt and pepper. Mix well. Blend in half-and-half. Stir in potatoes. Cover. Microwave at 70% (Medium High) for 20 to 26 minutes, or until potatoes are tender, stirring twice. Let stand, covered, for 5 minutes. Garnish with parsley.

Eggplant Au Gratin

Eleonora E. Svelti
Bayomon, Puerto Rico

1 medium eggplant, about 1½ lbs., peeled and cut into ½-inch cubes
1 medium tomato, seeded and chopped
1 medium onion, chopped
1 clove garlic, minced
¼ cup water
2 tablespoons butter or margarine
¼ cup milk
1 egg, slightly beaten
1 teaspoon salt
¼ cup grated Parmesan cheese
¼ cup seasoned dry bread crumbs
1 teaspoon dried parsley flakes

4 to 6 servings

In 2-quart casserole, combine eggplant, tomato, onion, garlic and water. Cover. Microwave at High for 10 to 15 minutes, or until eggplant is tender, stirring twice. Let stand, covered, for 5 minutes. Drain thoroughly. Set aside.

Place butter in 2-cup measure. Microwave at High for 45 seconds to 1 minute, or until butter melts. Blend in milk, egg and salt. Stir into eggplant mixture. In small mixing bowl, combine cheese, bread crumbs and parsley. Mix well. Sprinkle over eggplant mixture. Microwave, uncovered, at High for 5 to 6 minutes, or until set, rotating casserole once.

Mexican Seasoned Potatoes

Brenda Lee Moser
West Lawn, Pennsylvania

- 4 medium baking potatoes (8 oz. each)
- ¼ cup butter or margarine
- 1 tablespoon instant minced onion
- ½ teaspoon chili powder
- ½ teaspoon dried oregano leaves
- ¼ teaspoon ground cumin

6 to 8 servings

Cut each potato lengthwise into 4 equal wedges. Set aside. Place butter in 10-inch square casserole. Microwave at High for 1 to 1½ minutes, or until butter melts. Add potatoes, turning to coat with butter. In small bowl, combine remaining ingredients. Sprinkle over potatoes. Cover. Microwave at High for 14 to 18 minutes, or until potatoes are tender, rearranging potatoes twice. Let stand, covered, for 5 minutes.

Potatoes Purée Au Gratin ▲

Pat Kelsey
Davie, Florida

- 2 tablespoons butter or margarine
- 2 tablespoons water
- 3 cups peeled sliced potatoes, ⅛ inch thick
- ½ cup half-and-half
- ½ teaspoon salt
- ⅛ teaspoon hot pepper sauce
- ¼ cup grated Parmesan cheese
- 2 egg whites, stiffly beaten Grated Parmesan cheese

4 to 6 servings

In 1-quart casserole, combine butter, water and potatoes. Cover. Microwave at High for 9 to 12 minutes, or until potatoes are tender, stirring once. Add half-and-half, salt and hot pepper sauce. Beat with electric mixer until smooth. Mix in cheese. Fold in egg whites. Spoon into 1-quart soufflé dish or casserole. Microwave at 70% (Medium High) for 6 to 9 minutes, or until top appears dry and set, rotating dish twice. Sprinkle lightly with Parmesan cheese. Place under preheated broiler 3 to 4 inches from heat, until browned, 2 to 3 minutes.

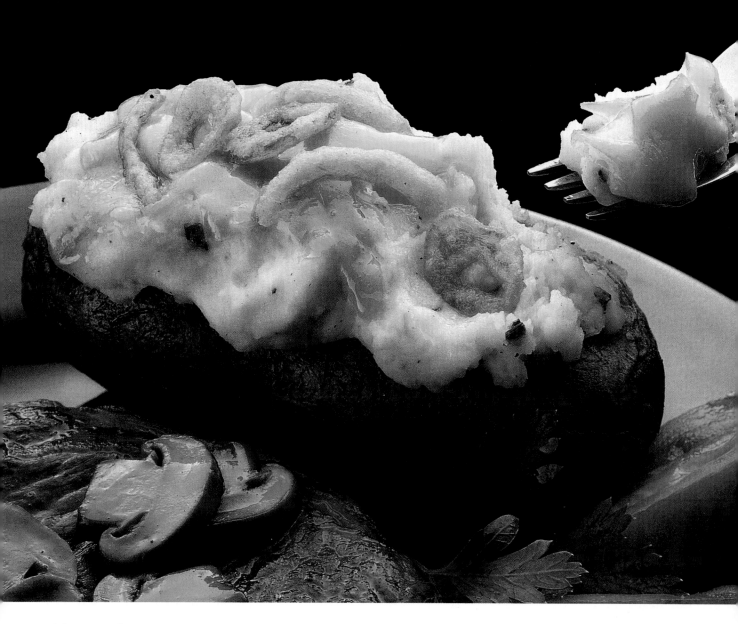

Elegant Stuffed Baked Potatoes

Mrs. Tally Orange
Paw Paw, Michigan

4 medium baking potatoes (8 oz. each)

¾ cup small curd cottage cheese

¼ cup butter or margarine, cut up

2 tablespoons milk

1 tablespoon freeze-dried chives

1 teaspoon seasoned salt

¼ teaspoon pepper

¼ cup shredded Cheddar cheese

¼ cup canned French fried onions

4 servings

Pierce potatoes with fork. Arrange in circular pattern on paper towel in microwave oven. Microwave at High for 10 to 14 minutes, or until tender, turning potatoes over and rearranging after half the time. Wrap each potato in foil. Let stand for 10 minutes. Cut thin slice from top of each potato. Scoop out pulp, leaving about ¼-inch shell. Place pulp in medium mixing bowl. Arrange shells on paper towel-lined plate. Set aside. Add cottage cheese, butter, milk, chives, seasoned salt and pepper to potato pulp. Beat with electric mixer until smooth and fluffy. Spoon mixture into potato shells. Microwave at High for 2 to 3 minutes, or until hot. Sprinkle each potato with cheese and onions. Microwave at High for 1½ to 2½ minutes, or until cheese melts, rotating plate once.

Creamed Spinach Casserole

Patricia Johnson
Mission Viejo, California

- 2 pkgs. (10 oz. each) frozen chopped spinach
- 3 tablespoons butter or margarine
- 3 tablespoons all-purpose flour
- ½ teaspoon salt
- ¼ teaspoon pepper
- 1¼ cups milk
- 2 hard-cooked eggs, chopped
- 2 slices whole wheat bread, toasted and cut into ½-inch cubes
- 1 tablespoon grated Parmesan cheese

4 to 6 servings

Unwrap spinach and place on plate. Microwave at High for 5 to 7 minutes, or until defrosted. Let stand for 5 minutes. Drain thoroughly, pressing to remove excess moisture. Set aside. Place butter in 4-cup measure. Microwave at High for 1 to 1¼ minutes, or until butter melts. Stir in flour, salt and pepper. Blend in milk. Microwave at High for 4 to 5 minutes, or until mixture thickens and bubbles, stirring 2 or 3 times. Stir in eggs. In 1½-quart casserole, layer half of spinach and half of white sauce. Repeat once. Top with toast cubes. Sprinkle with Parmesan cheese. Microwave at 70% (Medium High) for 6 to 10 minutes, or until heated through, rotating once.

Golden Potatoes ▲

Jana L. Bradley
Frontenac, Kansas

- 4 cups peeled sliced potatoes, ⅛ inch thick
- 1 medium onion, thinly sliced, separated into rings
- 2 tablespoons water
- 1 can (10¾ oz.) condensed cream of mushroom soup
- ½ cup shredded Cheddar cheese
- ½ cup dairy sour cream
- ¼ cup milk
- ½ teaspoon salt
- ¼ to ½ teaspoon curry powder
- ⅛ teaspoon pepper

4 to 6 servings

In 1½-quart casserole, combine potatoes, onion and water. Cover. Microwave at High for 9 to 12 minutes, or until potatoes are tender, stirring twice. In small mixing bowl, blend soup, cheese, sour cream, milk, salt, curry powder and pepper. Pour over potatoes. Mix well. Re-cover. Reduce power to 70% (Medium High). Microwave for 3 to 5 minutes, or until cheese melts, stirring once.

Summary Squash Bake

Summer Squash Bake

Robin R. Dunn
Herndon, Virginia

A favorite Southern-style recipe.

1½ lbs. summer squash, cut
    into ¼-inch slices
2 tablespoons butter or
    margarine
½ cup evaporated milk
2 eggs, beaten
1 tablespoon all-purpose flour
1 teaspoon baking powder
1 teaspoon grated onion
½ teaspoon salt
½ teaspoon sugar
    Dash pepper

Topping:
2 tablespoons butter or
    margarine
⅓ cup seasoned dry bread
    crumbs
¼ cup grated Parmesan
    cheese
2 teaspoons dried parsley
    flakes

6 to 8 servings

How to Microwave Summer Squash Bake

Combine squash and butter
in 1½-quart casserole. Cover.
Microwave at High for 14 to 18
minutes, or until squash is very
tender, stirring once. Let stand,
covered, for 5 minutes. Mash.
Set aside.

Blend evaporated milk, eggs,
flour, baking powder, onion,
salt, sugar and pepper in
2-cup measure. Stir into mashed
squash. Reduce power to 70%
(Medium High). Microwave,
uncovered, for 6 to 8 minutes,
or until set, stirring twice.

Place butter in small mixing
bowl. Microwave at High for
45 seconds to 1 minute, or until
butter melts. Stir in remaining
topping ingredients until
moistened. Sprinkle evenly over
squash mixture. Microwave at
70% (Medium High) for
3 minutes.

Creamy
Squash Casserole

Kathy Ferguson
Walnut Creek, California

1 lb. summer squash, cut into ¼-inch slices
1 lb. zucchini, cut into ¼-inch slices
¼ cup chopped onion
¼ cup butter or margarine
2 cups herb seasoned stuffing mix
1 can (10¾ oz.) condensed cream of chicken soup
1 cup shredded carrots
1 cup dairy sour cream
½ teaspoon salt
¼ teaspoon pepper

8 to 10 servings

In 10-inch square casserole, combine summer squash, zucchini and onion. Cover. Microwave at High for 7 to 8 minutes, or until vegetables are tender-crisp, stirring twice. Set aside. Place butter in small mixing bowl. Microwave at High for 1¼ to 1½ minutes, or until butter melts. Stir in stuffing mix until moistened. Set aside.

In small mixing bowl, blend soup, carrots, sour cream, salt and pepper. Stir into squash and onion mixture. Mix well. Sprinkle evenly with stuffing mixture. Reduce power to 70% (Medium High). Microwave, uncovered, for 12 to 18 minutes, or until hot and bubbly, rotating casserole once.

Zucchini Casserole

A tasty way to use excess zucchini from your garden.

Donna Champagne
Niagara, Wisconsin

2 slices bacon, cut up
2 cups chopped zucchini
1 can (16 oz.) stewed
  tomatoes
1 cup seasoned croutons
½ cup chopped green pepper
⅛ teaspoon garlic salt
2 tablespoons grated
  Parmesan cheese

  4 to 6 servings

Place bacon in 1½-quart casserole. Microwave at High for 2 to 3 minutes, or until brown and crisp, stirring once. Drain. Stir in zucchini, tomatoes, croutons, green pepper and garlic salt. Mix well. Cover. Microwave at High for 10 to 15 minutes, or until zucchini is tender, stirring once. Sprinkle with Parmesan cheese. Microwave, uncovered, at High for 1 to 2 minutes, or until cheese melts.

Au Gratin Vegetables

Cheri A. Olson
Apple Valley, Minnesota

1 cup fresh broccoli flowerets
1 cup fresh cauliflowerets
1 cup sliced fresh mushrooms
⅓ cup sliced carrot, ⅛ inch
   thick
⅓ cup finely chopped onion
1 tablespoon water
2 tablespoons butter or
   margarine
2 tablespoons all-purpose flour
½ teaspoon salt
⅛ teaspoon pepper
⅔ cup milk
½ cup finely shredded sharp
   Cheddar cheese

4 servings

In 1-quart pyroceram casserole, combine broccoli, cauliflower, mushrooms, carrot, onion and water. Cover. Microwave at High for 5 to 7 minutes, or until vegetables are tender-crisp, stirring once. Set aside.

Place butter in 2-cup measure. Microwave at High for 45 seconds to 1 minute, or until butter melts. Stir in flour, salt and pepper. Blend in milk. Microwave at High for 2 to 3 minutes, or until mixture thickens and bubbles, stirring after every minute. Stir hot mixture into vegetables. Sprinkle with cheese. Place under broiler until cheese melts, if desired.

Vegetable Delight ▶

Janice A. Clay
Salem, Massachusetts

2 tablespoons butter or
   margarine
1 cup sliced zucchini, ¼ inch
   thick
½ cup sliced celery, ¼ inch
   thick
½ cup chopped onion
½ cup chopped green pepper
½ cup sliced carrot, ⅛ inch
   thick
1 can (28 oz.) whole tomatoes,
   drained and cut up
1 can (4 oz.) sliced
   mushrooms, drained
½ teaspoon salt
½ teaspoon dried oregano
   leaves
½ teaspoon dried basil leaves
¼ teaspoon dried thyme leaves

6 to 8 servings

In 2-quart casserole, combine
butter, zucchini, celery, onion,
green pepper and carrot. Cover.
Microwave at High for 6 to 10
minutes, or until zucchini is
tender, stirring once.

Stir in tomatoes, mushrooms,
salt, oregano, basil and thyme.
Re-cover. Reduce power to
70% (Medium High). Microwave
for 5 to 8 minutes, or until flavors
are blended, stirring once.

Barley-Vegetable Casserole

Barbara S. Scholl
Lancaster, Ohio

2 tablespoons vegetable oil
¾ cup sliced fresh
   mushrooms
½ cup chopped celery
1 medium onion, chopped
1 clove garlic, minced
1 can (16 oz.) whole
   tomatoes

1½ cups ready-to-serve
   chicken broth
1 cup quick-cooking barley
⅛ teaspoon pepper
2 tablespoons grated
   Parmesan cheese
1 teaspoon snipped fresh
   parsley

4 to 6 servings

In 3-quart casserole, combine oil, mushrooms, celery, onion and
garlic. Cover. Microwave at High for 4 to 5 minutes, or until vegetables are tender, stirring twice. Stir in tomatoes, broth, barley and
pepper. Re-cover. Microwave at High for 20 to 25 minutes, or until
liquid is absorbed and barley is tender, stirring after every 5
minutes. Sprinkle with Parmesan cheese and parsley. Let stand,
covered, for 10 minutes.

Stuffing

Fluffy French Bread Stuffing

Garda Slorp
Hayden Lake, Idaho

6 tablespoons butter or margarine
¾ cup sliced celery, ⅛ inch thick
1 medium onion, finely chopped
⅓ cup snipped fresh parsley
1 teaspoon dried crushed sage leaves
½ lb. cubed French bread, ¾-inch cubes, about 8 cups
¼ cup chopped walnuts
1 can (10¾ oz.) condensed cream of chicken soup
2 eggs, beaten
¼ cup milk

6 to 8 servings

In large mixing bowl, combine butter, celery, onion, parsley and sage. Cover with plastic wrap. Microwave at High for 5 to 7 minutes, or until celery is tender, stirring once. Mix in bread cubes and walnuts. In small mixing bowl, blend soup, eggs and milk. Pour over bread mixture. Stir to moisten. Spoon into 1½-quart casserole. Microwave at 70% (Medium High) for 10 to 16 minutes, or until heated through and mixture is set, stirring twice.

Sausage & Apple Stuffing

Susanne Adams
Livingston, Montana

½ lb. pork sausage
¼ cup butter or margarine
1⅓ cups sliced fresh
  mushrooms
 1 medium apple, chopped
½ cup chopped celery
½ cup chopped onion
½ teaspoon salt
½ teaspoon poultry seasoning
½ teaspoon dried crushed
  sage leaves
¼ teaspoon pepper
 5 cups unseasoned whole
  wheat and white croutons
¾ cup ready-to-serve chicken
  broth

6 to 8 servings

How to Microwave Sausage & Apple Stuffing

Crumble sausage into 1-quart casserole. Cover. Microwave at High for 3 to 6 minutes, or until sausage is no longer pink, stirring once to break apart. Drain. Set aside.

Combine butter, mushrooms, apple, celery and onion in 2-quart casserole. Cover. Microwave at High for 7 to 9 minutes, or until celery is tender, stirring once. Stir in sausage and remaining ingredients, except chicken broth.

Pour broth evenly over croutons and vegetables. Stir to moisten. Re-cover. Microwave at High for 3 to 5 minutes, or until heated through, stirring once.

Rice

Rice Oregano

Sharon Allen
Wichita, Kansas

2 cups hot water
1 cup uncooked long grain white rice
¼ cup finely chopped onion
2 tablespoons butter or margarine
4 teaspoons instant chicken bouillon granules
½ teaspoon dried oregano leaves
⅛ teaspoon pepper

6 servings

In 2-quart casserole, combine all ingredients. Mix well. Cover. Microwave at High for 5 minutes. Reduce power to 50% (Medium). Microwave for 13 to 19 minutes, or until liquid is absorbed and rice is tender. Let stand, covered, for 5 minutes. Stir with fork.

Spanish Rice with Shrimp

Debra Kay Hampton
Aiea, Hawaii

1 can (16 oz.) stewed
   tomatoes
1½ cups water
⅔ cup uncooked long grain
   white rice
⅓ cup finely chopped onion
¼ cup chopped celery
3 tablespoons tomato paste
1 teaspoon salt

1 teaspoon sugar
1 teaspoon instant chicken
   bouillon granules
½ teaspoon dried oregano
   leaves
¼ to ½ teaspoon garlic
   powder
1 can (4¼ oz.) small shrimp,
   rinsed and drained

6 to 8 servings

In 2-quart casserole, combine
all ingredients, except shrimp.
Mix well. Cover. Microwave at
High for 10 minutes. Reduce
power to 50% (Medium). Microwave for 28 to 35 minutes, or
until liquid is absorbed and rice
is tender. Stir in shrimp. Let
stand, covered, for 5 minutes.

119

Fresh Fruit-topped Cheesecake

Breads

◄ Chocolate-Banana Nut Bread

Linda Kay Jerew
Richwood, Ohio

¼ cup granola cereal
3 tablespoons milk
¼ cup butter or margarine
3 squares (1 oz. each)
    semisweet chocolate
½ cup dairy sour cream
½ cup mashed ripe banana
1 egg
1¼ cups all-purpose flour
½ cup sugar
⅓ cup chopped nuts
½ teaspoon baking powder
½ teaspoon baking soda
½ teaspoon salt

1 loaf

Line bottom of 9 × 5-inch loaf dish with wax paper. Set aside. In small bowl, combine granola and milk. Set aside. In medium mixing bowl, combine butter and chocolate. Microwave at 50% (Medium) for 3 to 4 minutes, or until chocolate melts and can be stirred smooth, stirring once. Cool slightly. Add remaining ingredients and granola and milk mixture. Beat at high speed of electric mixer for 1 minute, scraping bowl occasionally. Spread batter evenly into prepared dish. Shield ends with 2-inch strips of foil, covering 1 inch of batter and molding remainder around handles of dish.

Place dish on saucer in microwave oven. Microwave at 50% (Medium) for 9 minutes, rotating dish after every 4½ minutes. Remove foil. Increase power to High. Microwave for 3 to 7 minutes, or until top appears dry and loaf starts to pull away from sides, rotating dish once. Let stand on counter for 5 to 10 minutes. Invert onto wire rack. Cool.

◄ Whole Grain Muffins

Kandace A. Beale
Kersey, Pennsylvania

A smaller recipe for a family of two.

1 large shredded wheat
    biscuit, crumbled
½ cup quick-cooking
    rolled oats
⅓ cup 100% bran cereal
⅔ cup milk
1 egg, slightly beaten
2 tablespoons vegetable oil
2 tablespoons honey
1 tablespoon packed brown
    sugar
⅓ cup all-purpose flour
½ teaspoon baking soda
⅛ teaspoon salt

Topping:
1 tablespoon granulated sugar
¼ teaspoon ground cinnamon

6 muffins

Line six muffin cups with two paper baking cups in each. Set aside. In medium mixing bowl, combine shredded wheat, rolled oats and bran cereal. Pour milk over mixture. Mix well. Stir in egg, oil, honey and brown sugar. Mix well. In small bowl, combine flour, baking soda and salt. Add flour mixture to cereal mixture, stirring just until dry ingredients are moistened. Fill each paper-lined muffin cup half full. Microwave at High for 3½ to 5½ minutes, or until tops spring back when touched lightly, rotating cups twice. (Some moist spots will remain.) Remove from muffin cups to wire rack. In small bowl, mix topping ingredients. Sprinkle topping on warm muffins.

Cornbread Ring

Based on grandmother's recipe.

Victoria E. Inscho
Etters, Pennsylvania

Vegetable cooking spray
¼ cup cornflake crumbs
1 cup all-purpose flour
1 cup yellow cornmeal
½ cup sugar
1 teaspoon baking soda
¼ cup butter or margarine
1 egg, slightly beaten
1 cup buttermilk

8 servings

Spray 9-inch ring dish with vegetable cooking spray. Sprinkle with cornflake crumbs. Tilt dish to coat. Set aside. In medium mixing bowl, combine flour, cornmeal, sugar and baking soda. Set aside. Place butter in small bowl. Microwave at High for 1¼ to 1½ minutes, or until butter melts. Add butter, egg and buttermilk to cornmeal mixture. Stir just until dry ingredients are moistened. Pour batter evenly into prepared dish. Microwave at 50% (Medium) for 5 minutes, rotating dish after half the time. Increase power to High. Microwave for 4 to 7 minutes, or until top springs back when touched lightly, rotating dish after every 2 minutes. Let stand on counter for 5 minutes. Invert onto serving plate. Serve warm.

Apple-Wheat Coffee Cake

Carol A. Bodenhorn
Monongahela, Pennsylvania

 1 cup whole wheat flour
 ¾ cup packed brown sugar
 ½ cup all-purpose flour
 ½ cup butter or margarine
 ¾ teaspoon baking powder
 ½ teaspoon salt
 ⅔ cup milk
 1 egg, slightly beaten
 1 medium apple, peeled,
    cored and thinly sliced
 ¼ cup chopped walnuts
 1 teaspoon ground cinnamon

9 servings

In large mixing bowl, combine whole wheat flour, brown sugar and all-purpose flour. Set aside. Place butter on small plate. Microwave at 30% (Medium Low) for 15 seconds to 1 minute, or until softened, checking after every 15 seconds. Cut butter into flour mixture until coarse crumbs form. Reserve 1 cup flour and butter mixture. Set aside. Add baking powder, salt, milk and egg to remaining mixture. Stir just until dry ingredients are moistened. Spread batter evenly into 9-inch square baking dish. Arrange apple slices on batter. Add walnuts and cinnamon to reserved flour and butter mixture. Mix well. Sprinkle over apple slices. Shield corners of dish with foil.

Place dish on saucer in microwave oven. Microwave at 50% (Medium) for 9 minutes, rotating dish after every 3 minutes. Remove foil. Increase power to High. Microwave for 3 to 6 minutes, or until center springs back when touched lightly and no uncooked batter remains on the bottom, rotating once. Let stand on counter for 5 minutes. Serve warm.

Whole Wheat Beer Bread

William R. Buziak
Miami, Florida

   2 tablespoons cornflake
       crumbs
1¾ cups whole wheat flour
   1 cup all-purpose flour
   ¼ cup 100% bran cereal
   ¼ cup grated Parmesan
       cheese
   2 teaspoons baking powder
   1 teaspoon garlic salt
   1 teaspoon dried oregano
       leaves
   1 teaspoon dried parsley
       flakes
   1 can (12 oz.) beer, room
       temperature
   ⅓ cup vegetable oil
   1 egg, beaten
   2 tablespoons honey

1 loaf

Grease 9 × 5-inch loaf dish. Sprinkle with cornflake crumbs. Tilt dish to coat. Set aside. In medium mixing bowl, combine whole wheat and all-purpose flours, cereal, cheese, baking powder, garlic salt, oregano and parsley. Set aside. In small mixing bowl, blend remaining ingredients. Pour into flour mixture. Beat well. Spread batter evenly into prepared dish. Shield ends with 2-inch strips of foil, covering 1 inch of batter and molding remainder around handles of dish.

Place dish on saucer in microwave oven. Microwave at 50% (Medium) for 8 minutes, rotating dish after every 4 minutes. Remove foil. Increase power to High. Microwave for 5 to 7 minutes, or until center springs back when touched lightly and top appears dry, rotating dish once. Let stand on counter for 5 minutes. Invert onto wire rack. Serve warm with butter and honey.

Raisin-Spice Loaf

This loaf has no eggs, milk or butter.

Mrs. Constance H. Reagor
Bella Vista, Arkansas

2 tablespoons graham cracker
  crumbs
1 cup raisins
1 cup packed brown sugar
1 cup hot strong coffee
⅓ cup vegetable shortening
1 teaspoon ground cinnamon
½ teaspoon ground cloves
¼ teaspoon ground nutmeg
¼ teaspoon vanilla
2 cups all-purpose flour
1 teaspoon baking soda
1 teaspoon baking powder
½ teaspoon salt

1 loaf

Grease 9 × 5-inch loaf dish. Sprinkle with graham cracker crumbs. Tilt dish to coat. Set aside. Grind raisins in meat grinder or place in food processor bowl. Process until raisins form a ball and clean sides of bowl. In 4-cup measure, combine raisins, brown sugar, coffee, shortening, cinnamon, cloves, nutmeg and vanilla. Mix well. Microwave at High for 3 to 4 minutes, or until shortening melts, stirring after every minute. Set aside. In medium mixing bowl, combine flour, baking soda, baking powder and salt. Add raisin mixture. Beat at medium speed of electric mixer for 1 minute, scraping bowl occasionally. Spread batter evenly into prepared dish. Shield ends with 2-inch strips of foil, covering 1 inch of batter and molding remainder around handles of dish.

Place dish on saucer in microwave oven. Microwave at 70% (Medium High) for 8 minutes, rotating dish after half the time. Remove foil. Microwave at 70% (Medium High) for 4 to 7 minutes, or until top appears dry and no uncooked batter remains on the bottom, rotating dish once. Let stand on counter for 5 to 10 minutes. Invert onto wire rack. Cool.

Cakes

◄ Black Walnut Cake

Mrs. Muriel B. Berger
Phoenixville, Pennsylvania

1¾ cups all-purpose flour
1⅓ cups granulated sugar
1 cup ground black walnuts
1 tablespoon baking powder
½ teaspoon salt
⅔ cup shortening
1 cup milk
2 eggs
2 egg whites
1 teaspoon vanilla

Frosting:
¾ cup butter or margarine
3 cups powdered sugar
1½ teaspoons vanilla
⅛ teaspoon salt
3 to 4 tablespoons
  half-and-half or milk
¾ cup ground walnuts
  Black walnut halves
  (optional)

8 servings

Line bottom of two 9-inch round cake dishes with wax paper. Set aside. In medium mixing bowl, combine all cake ingredients. Beat at low speed of electric mixer until moistened. Beat at medium speed for 2 minutes, scraping bowl occasionally. Divide batter evenly between prepared dishes.

Place one dish at a time on saucer in microwave oven. Microwave at 70% (Medium High) for 5 minutes. Rotate dish half turn. Increase power to High. Microwave for 1½ to 6½ minutes, or until center springs back when touched lightly and no uncooked batter remains on the bottom, rotating dish 2 or 3 times. Let stand on counter for 5 minutes. Invert onto wire rack. Repeat with second layer. Cool cake completely.

Place butter in medium mixing bowl. Microwave at 30% (Medium Low) for 30 seconds to 1 minute, or until softened, checking after every 15 seconds. Add powdered sugar, vanilla, salt and 3 table-spoons half-and-half. Beat at low speed of electric mixer until smooth, adding half-and-half until desired spreading consistency. Stir in ground walnuts. Place one cake layer on serving plate. Spread with one-third of frosting. Top with second layer. Frost top and sides of cake with remaining frosting. Garnish with walnuts.

Whiskey Cake

Barbara M. Wingender
Toms River, New Jersey

Decorate cake with cherries for Christmas or red candied hearts for Valentine's Day.

2 tablespoons graham cracker crumbs
1 pkg. (18¼ oz.) yellow cake mix
1 cup water
⅓ cup vegetable oil
¼ cup whiskey
3 eggs
1 cup ground walnuts

Glaze:
½ cup sugar
¼ cup butter or margarine
¼ cup whiskey

12 servings

Grease 12-cup fluted ring dish. Sprinkle with graham cracker crumbs. Tilt dish to coat. Set aside. In large mixing bowl, combine cake mix, water, oil, whiskey and eggs. Beat at low speed of electric mixer until moistened. Beat at medium speed for 2 minutes, scraping bowl occasionally. Stir in walnuts. Pour batter into prepared dish.

Place dish on saucer in microwave oven. Microwave at 50% (Medium) for 5 minutes. Rotate dish half turn. Increase power to High. Microwave for 7 to 11 minutes, or just until cake starts to pull away from sides and wooden pick inserted in center comes out clean, rotating dish after every 4 minutes. Let stand on counter for 10 minutes. Pierce cake thoroughly with thin knife. Let stand while preparing glaze.

In 2-cup measure, combine all glaze ingredients. Microwave at 50% (Medium) for 3 minutes, or until mixture boils, stirring after every minute. Pour glaze slowly over hot cake. Chill cake for at least 3 hours. Loosen edges. Invert onto serving plate. Serve with French vanilla ice cream or whipped cream.

Chocolate Chip Zucchini Cake

Cindy Hosfelt
Shippensburg, Pennsylvania

Try peanut butter chips instead of chocolate chips for a new taste.

¼ cup butter or margarine
1 cup sugar
¼ cup vegetable oil
1 cup all-purpose flour
2 tablespoons cocoa
½ teaspoon baking soda
¼ teaspoon baking powder
¼ teaspoon ground cinnamon
1 cup shredded zucchini
¼ cup buttermilk
1 egg
½ teaspoon vanilla
6 tablespoons semisweet
   chocolate chips

Frosting:
2 tablespoons all-purpose flour
½ cup milk
2 tablespoons butter or
   margarine
½ cup sugar
   Dash salt
¼ cup vegetable shortening
½ teaspoon vanilla

9 to 12 servings

Place butter in medium mixing bowl. Microwave at 30% (Medium Low) for 15 to 45 seconds, or until softened, checking after every 15 seconds. Add sugar and oil. Beat at medium speed of electric mixer until light and fluffy. Add remaining cake ingredients, except chocolate chips. Beat at low speed until moistened. Beat at medium speed for 1 minute, scraping bowl occasionally. Stir in chocolate chips. Spread batter into 9-inch square baking dish. Shield corners of dish with triangles of foil.

Place dish on saucer in microwave oven. Microwave at 50% (Medium) for 6 minutes. Rotate dish half turn. Remove foil. Increase power to High. Microwave for 5 to 10 minutes, or until top appears dry and center springs back when touched lightly, rotating dish twice. Let stand on counter. Cool completely.

Place flour in medium mixing bowl. Blend in milk. Microwave at High for 2 to 2½ minutes, or until mixture becomes very thick and paste-like, stirring with whisk after every minute. Chill for 45 minutes. Place butter in small bowl. Microwave at 30% (Medium Low) for 15 to 30 seconds, or until softened. Add butter and remaining frosting ingredients to flour mixture. Beat at high speed for 3 minutes, or until light and fluffy. Spread frosting over top of cooled cake.

Chocolate Brownie Cake

Mrs. Patricia M. Birdsall
Kenosha, Wisconsin

2 tablespoons cocoa
½ cup water
¼ cup vegetable oil
1 cup all-purpose flour
1 cup granulated sugar
½ teaspoon salt
½ teaspoon baking soda
½ teaspoon ground cinnamon
¼ cup buttermilk
1 egg
½ teaspoon vanilla

Frosting:
¼ cup butter or margarine
3 tablespoons milk
2 tablespoons cocoa
⅛ teaspoon salt
1⅔ cups powdered sugar
½ cup chopped nuts

9 to 12 servings

Place cocoa in 2-cup measure. Gradually blend in water. Stir in oil. Microwave at High for 2½ to 3 minutes, or until mixture boils. Set aside. In medium mixing bowl, combine flour, sugar, salt, baking soda and cinnamon. Add hot cocoa mixture. Beat at low speed of electric mixer until moistened. Add buttermilk, egg and vanilla. Beat at medium speed for 2 minutes, scraping bowl occasionally. Pour batter into 9-inch square baking dish. Shield corners of dish with triangles of foil.

Place dish on saucer in microwave oven. Microwave at 70% (Medium High) for 7 minutes, rotating dish once. Remove foil. Microwave at 70% (Medium High) for 3 to 9 minutes, or until top appears dry and center springs back when touched lightly, rotating dish once or twice. Let stand on counter for 10 minutes.

In 4-cup measure, combine butter, milk, cocoa and salt. Microwave at High for 2½ to 3 minutes, or until mixture boils, stirring after every minute. Beat in powdered sugar until smooth. Stir in nuts. Spread frosting over top of hot cake. Serve warm or cool.

Fresh Apple Cake

Brenda Gail Lynn
Haines City, Florida

⅔ cup all-purpose flour
½ cup packed brown sugar
½ teaspoon baking soda
½ teaspoon ground cinnamon, optional
¼ teaspoon salt
⅓ cup shortening
2 eggs
1 teaspoon vanilla
2 cups peeled chopped apples
¾ cup chopped nuts

Glaze:
⅓ cup powdered sugar
1½ to 2 teaspoons half-and-half

6 to 8 servings

Line bottom of 9-inch round cake dish with wax paper. Set aside. In medium mixing bowl, combine cake ingredients, except apples and nuts. Beat at low speed of electric mixer until blended. Beat at high speed for 1 minute, scraping bowl occasionally. Stir in apples and nuts. Spread batter evenly into prepared dish.

Place dish on saucer in microwave oven. Microwave at 70% (Medium High) for 5 minutes. Rotate dish half turn. Increase power to High. Microwave for 3 to 8 minutes, or until top appears dry and center springs back when touched lightly, rotating dish once. Let stand on counter for 5 minutes. Invert onto wire rack. Cool completely.

In small bowl, blend powdered sugar and half-and-half. Drizzle glaze over cake.

Pistachio Swirl Cake

Holly Eash
Cape Coral, Florida

1 cup finely chopped pecans
½ cup sugar
1 tablespoon ground
   cinnamon
1 pkg. (18¼ oz.) white cake
   mix
1 pkg. (3½ oz.) instant
   pistachio pudding and
   pie filling
4 eggs
1 cup dairy sour cream
¾ cup water
¼ cup vegetable oil
1 teaspoon vanilla

      12 to 15 servings

In small mixing bowl, combine pecans, sugar and cinnamon. Mix well. Set aside. Grease 12-cup fluted ring dish. Sprinkle with ¼ cup pecan mixture. Tilt dish to coat. Set aside. Reserve remaining pecan mixture. In large mixing bowl, combine remaining ingredients. Beat at low speed of electric mixer until moistened. Beat at medium speed for 2 minutes, scraping bowl occasionally. Alternate layers of batter and reserved pecan mixture in prepared dish. Swirl through batter and pecan mixture with knife.

Place dish on saucer in microwave oven. Microwave at 50% (Medium) for 10 minutes, rotating dish after every 5 minutes. Increase power to High. Microwave for 10 to 15 minutes, or just until cake starts to pull away from sides of dish, rotating dish after every 5 minutes. Let stand on counter for 15 minutes. Invert onto serving plate. Cool.

Pies

◄ Triple Delicious Strawberry Pie

An award-winning recipe in a local contest combines several types of strawberry pies.

Theta Nicholson
Bardwell, Kentucky

1 baked and cooled 9-inch pastry shell, below
⅓ cup chopped pecans
1 pkg. (8 oz.) cream cheese
2 cups prepared whipped topping
1 cup powdered sugar
¾ cup granulated sugar
2 tablespoons cornstarch
⅛ teaspoon salt
¾ cup water

2 tablespoons dry strawberry-flavored gelatin
1 teaspoon vanilla
2 drops red food coloring, optional
1 pint strawberries, hulled and sliced
Whole strawberries (optional)
Whipped topping (optional)

One 9-inch pie

Prepare pastry shell as directed. Sprinkle pecans over bottom of cooled pastry shell. Set aside. Place cream cheese in small mixing bowl. Microwave at 50% (Medium) for 1 to 1½ minutes, or until softened. Blend in whipped topping and powdered sugar. Spread over pecans in pastry shell. Chill for 1 hour.

In 4-cup measure, combine granulated sugar, cornstarch and salt. Blend in water. Microwave at High for 3½ to 4½ minutes, or until mixture is thickened and translucent, stirring after every minute. Stir in gelatin, vanilla and food coloring. Cover with plastic wrap. Chill for 2 hours. Stir in sliced strawberries. Spread over cream cheese mixture. Chill for 2 hours, or until set. Garnish with whole strawberries and whipped topping.

Harvest Gold Pie

Rev. Margaret Strodtz
Maynard, Iowa

1 baked and cooled 9-inch pastry shell, below
1 pkg. (3 oz.) egg custard mix
2 cups half-and-half
1 cup canned pumpkin
1 teaspoon pumpkin pie spice
Whipped topping (optional)

One 9-inch pie

Prepare pastry shell as directed. Set aside. Place custard mix in 2-quart measure. Blend in half-and-half. Microwave at High for 6½ to 10 minutes, or until mixture boils, stirring after every 2 minutes. Cool for 15 minutes, stirring occasionally. In small mixing bowl, combine pumpkin and pumpkin pie spice. Mix well. Blend pumpkin mixture into custard mixture. Pour filling into prepared pastry shell. Chill for at least 3 hours, or until set. Garnish with whipped topping.

One-Crust Pastry Shell

Staff Home Economists
Cy DeCosse Incorporated

1 cup all-purpose flour
½ teaspoon salt
⅓ cup shortening
2 tablespoons butter or margarine, cut up
2 to 4 tablespoons cold water

One 9-inch pastry shell

In medium mixing bowl, combine flour and salt. Cut in shortening and butter to form coarse crumbs. Sprinkle with water, 1 tablespoon at a time, mixing with fork until particles are moistened and cling together. Form dough into a ball. Roll out on lightly floured board at least 2 inches larger than inverted 9-inch pie plate. Ease into plate. Trim and flute edge. Prick thoroughly. Microwave at High for 5 to 7 minutes, or until pastry appears dry and opaque, rotating plate after every 2 minutes. Cool.

Or, preheat conventional oven to 400°F. Bake until light golden brown, 10 to 12 minutes.

Company Coconut Cream Pie

An elegant pie for dinner guests.

Mrs. Alyce D. Peiffer
York, Pennsylvania

Pastry:
1½ cups all-purpose flour
½ teaspoon salt
½ cup shortening
4 to 5 tablespoons cold water

Filling:
¾ cup sugar
6 tablespoons cornstarch
½ teaspoon salt
3½ cups milk
4 egg yolks, beaten
4½ teaspoons butter or
    margarine
1½ teaspoons vanilla
2 cups flaked coconut

Meringue:
4 egg whites
½ teaspoon cream of tartar
5 tablespoons sugar
¾ teaspoon vanilla

One 10-inch pie

In medium mixing bowl, combine flour and salt. Cut in shortening to form coarse crumbs. Sprinkle with water, 1 tablespoon at a time, mixing with fork until particles are moistened and cling together. Form dough into a ball. Roll out on lightly floured board at least 2 inches larger than inverted 10-inch deep dish pie plate. Ease into plate. Trim and flute edge. Prick thoroughly. Microwave at High for 5 to 8 minutes, or until pastry appears dry and opaque, rotating plate after every 2 minutes. Cool. Set aside.

In 2-quart measure, combine sugar, cornstarch and salt. Blend in milk. Microwave at High for 9 to 14 minutes, or until mixture comes to a rolling boil, stirring 3 times with whisk. Microwave at High for 1 minute. Blend small amount of hot mixture into egg yolks. Add back to hot mixture, stirring constantly. Reduce power to 70% (Medium High). Microwave for 1½ to 2 minutes, or until mixture thickens, stirring once or twice with whisk. Blend in butter and vanilla. Stir in coconut. Pour filling into cooled pastry shell.

Preheat conventional oven to 400°F. In large mixing bowl, combine egg whites and cream of tartar. Beat until foamy. Gradually add sugar, beating until stiff peaks form. Blend in vanilla. Spread meringue over hot filling, sealing to edge of pastry. Bake until lightly browned, 8 to 10 minutes. Cool. Chill for at least 6 hours before serving.

Red Apple Crisp Pie ▶

Linda L. Ilg
Worland, Wyoming

1 baked and cooled 9-inch
   pastry shell, page 135

Filling:
4 cups unpeeled grated red
   cooking apples
¾ cup granulated sugar
2 tablespoons all-purpose flour
¼ teaspoon ground cinnamon
⅛ teaspoon salt
1 tablespoon lemon juice

Topping:
⅓ cup packed brown sugar
⅓ cup all-purpose flour
⅛ teaspoon salt
3 tablespoons butter or
   margarine, cut up

One 9-inch pie

Prepare pastry shell as directed.
Set aside. In medium mixing
bowl, combine all filling ingredients. Mix well. Spoon filling
into prepared pastry shell.
Smooth top of filling.

Place pie plate on saucer in
microwave oven. Microwave at
70% (Medium High) for 20 to 25
minutes, or until center is hot,
rotating plate twice. In small
mixing bowl, combine brown
sugar, flour and salt. Cut in
butter to form fine crumbs.
Sprinkle topping evenly over
hot pie. Place under preheated
broiler 2 to 3 inches from heat,
until golden brown, about 2
minutes. Serve with ice cream.

Chocolate S'more Pie

Susanne Adams
Livingston, Montana

Graham Cracker Crust:
5 tablespoons butter or
   margarine
1⅓ cups graham cracker
   crumbs
2 tablespoons sugar

Filling:
1 bar (8 oz.) milk chocolate
   with almonds, broken into
   small pieces

16 large marshmallows
¼ cup milk
2½ cups prepared whipped
   topping
Whipped topping (optional)
Chocolate curls (optional)

One 9-inch pie

Place butter in 9-inch pie plate. Microwave at High for 1¼ to 1½
minutes, or until butter melts. Stir in graham cracker crumbs and
sugar. Mix well. Press mixture firmly against bottom and sides of
pie plate. Microwave at High for 1½ to 2 minutes, or until set,
rotating plate after 1 minute. Cool. Set aside.

Place chocolate pieces in 2-quart measure. Add marshmallows and
milk. Microwave at High for 2 to 3½ minutes, or until chocolate and
marshmallows melt, stirring after every minute. Cover. Chill for 45
minutes. Fold whipped topping into chocolate mixture. Pour filling
into prepared crust. Chill for at least 4 hours, or until set. Garnish
with whipped topping and chocolate curls.

Desserts

Fluffy Butter Pecan Cooler ▶

Chris Anderson
Negaunee, Michigan

Crust:

- 1 cup all-purpose flour
- ⅓ cup chopped pecans
- 3 tablespoons granulated sugar
- ½ cup butter or margarine, cut into ½-inch cubes

Filling:

- 1 pkg. (3 oz.) cream cheese
- 2½ cups prepared whipped topping, divided
- ½ cup powdered sugar
- 1 pkg. (3½ oz.) instant butter pecan pudding and pie filling
- 1½ cups milk
- ⅓ cup chopped pecans

9 servings

How to Microwave Fluffy Butter Pecan Cooler

Combine flour, pecans and sugar in medium mixing bowl. Add butter. Cut in butter at low speed of electric mixer to form coarse crumbs.

Press mixture firmly against bottom of 9-inch square baking dish. Place dish on saucer in microwave oven. Microwave at 70% (Medium High) for 6 to 8 minutes, or until crust appears dry and firm, rotating dish once. Cool. Set aside.

Place cream cheese in small mixing bowl. Microwave at 50% (Medium) for 30 to 45 seconds, or until softened. Blend in ½ cup whipped topping and powdered sugar. Mix well. Spread over cooled crust.

Fresh Fruit-topped Cheesecake

Penny Dunbar
Green Bay, Wisconsin

Crust:
　5　tablespoons butter or
　　　margarine
1⅓　cups graham cracker
　　　crumbs
　2　tablespoons sugar

Filling:
　1　pkg. (8 oz.) cream cheese
　½　cup sugar
　1　egg, slightly beaten
　1　tablespoon milk
　1　teaspoon vanilla

Topping:
　2　cups fresh fruit (sliced kiwi
　　　fruit, strawberries, peaches,
　　　dark sweet cherries or
　　　blueberries)

6 to 8 servings

Place butter in 9-inch pie plate. Microwave at High for 1¼ to 1½ minutes, or until butter melts. Stir in graham cracker crumbs and sugar. Mix well. Press mixture firmly against bottom and sides of pie plate. Microwave at High for 1½ to 2 minutes, or until set, rotating plate after 1 minute. Cool. Set aside.

Place cream cheese in 2-quart measure. Microwave at 50% (Medium) for 1½ to 3 minutes, or until softened. Add remaining filling ingredients. Beat at medium speed of electric mixer until well blended. Microwave at High for 2 to 3 minutes, or until mixture is very hot and starts to set, beating once with whisk. Pour filling into prepared crust.

Place pie plate on saucer in microwave oven. Microwave at 50% (Medium) for 4 to 9 minutes, or until center is almost set. Filling will become firm as it cools. Cool for 1 hour. Chill for at least 6 hours. Arrange or spoon topping over cheesecake.

Combine pudding mix and milk in medium mixing bowl. Beat at low speed for 1 to 2 minutes until blended. Pour over cream cheese layer.

Spread remaining 2 cups whipped topping over pudding. Sprinkle with pecans. Cover with plastic wrap. Chill for at least 3 hours.

Chocolate-Amaretto Cheesecake

Shirley J. Portouw
Steamboat Springs, Colorado

Crust:
- ¼ cup butter or margarine
- 1 cup graham cracker crumbs
- 2 tablespoons granulated sugar

Filling:
- 2 squares (1 oz. each) semisweet chocolate
- 2 pkgs. (8 oz. each) cream cheese
- ⅔ cup granulated sugar
- 4 eggs, slightly beaten
- 3 tablespoons amaretto liqueur
- 1 teaspoon vanilla
- ½ teaspoon almond extract

Topping:
- 2 tablespoons powdered sugar
- 1 tablespoon cocoa
- ½ cup dairy sour cream
- 1 teaspoon amaretto liqueur

8 to 10 servings

How to Microwave Chocolate-Amaretto Cheesecake

Place butter in 9-inch round baking dish. Microwave at High for 1¼ to 1½ minutes, or until butter melts. Stir in graham cracker crumbs and sugar. Mix well.

Press mixture firmly against bottom of dish. Microwave at High for 1½ to 2 minutes, or until set, rotating dish once. Set aside.

Place chocolate in custard cup. Microwave at 50% (Medium) for 3½ to 5 minutes, or until chocolate melts and can be stirred smooth, stirring once. Set aside. Place cream cheese in 2-quart measure. Microwave at 50% (Medium) for 2¼ to 4 minutes, or until softened. Blend in chocolate.

Add remaining filling ingredients. Beat at medium speed of electric mixer until well blended. Microwave at High for 4 to 5 minutes, or until mixture is very hot and starts to set, beating with whisk after every 2 minutes. Pour filling into prepared crust.

Place dish on saucer in microwave oven. Microwave at 50% (Medium) for 7 to 15 minutes, or until center is almost set, rotating dish twice. Filling will become firm as it cools. Cool for 1 hour.

Combine powdered sugar and cocoa in small mixing bowl. Blend in sour cream and amaretto until smooth. Spread topping over cheesecake. Chill for at least 8 hours, or overnight. Garnish with chocolate curls, if desired.

English Trifle

Marge Francis
Diamond Bar, California

1 pkg. (3⅛ oz.) vanilla pudding and pie filling
2 cups half-and-half
1 cup whipping cream
2 tablespoons sugar
2 tablespoons dark rum

1 jar (12 oz.) seedless red raspberry jam
1 pkg. (10¾ oz.) frozen pound cake, defrosted
1 pkg. (3 oz.) ladyfingers, split
¼ cup sherry
¼ cup brandy

2 tablespoons water
1 tablespoon lemon juice
2 peaches, sliced
2 bananas, sliced
1 peach, sliced (optional)
2 tablespoons sliced almonds (optional)

10 to 12 servings

How to Microwave English Trifle

Place pudding mix in 1½-quart casserole. Blend in half-and-half. Microwave at High for 2 minutes. Beat with whisk. Microwave at High for 3 to 6 minutes, or until mixture boils, stirring 2 or 3 times with whisk. Place sheet of plastic wrap directly on surface of pudding. Cool completely.

Place whipping cream in medium mixing bowl. Beat, gradually adding sugar, until soft peaks form. Blend rum into pudding. Fold whipped cream into pudding. Set aside. Place jam in small mixing bowl. Microwave at High for 1½ to 2½ minutes, or until hot. Stir until melted. Set aside.

Cut pound cake into 20 slices, about ¼ inch thick. Spread jam on one side of each slice of pound cake. Arrange half of pound cake slices, jam-side up, in bottom of 4-quart trifle dish or clear straight-sided bowl.

Spread or brush jam on cut-side of ladyfingers. Arrange ladyfingers along sides with jam toward center of dish. In 1-cup measure, blend sherry and brandy. Pour half of sherry mixture evenly over ladyfingers and pound cake. Spread one-third of pudding over pound cake.

Blend water and lemon juice in small bowl. Dip peach and banana slices in lemon mixture to prevent browning. Shake off excess. Arrange half of peach and banana slices over pudding. Top with remaining half of pound cake slices. Pour remaining sherry mixture evenly over pound cake.

Spread one-third of pudding over pound cake. Top with remaining half of peach and banana slices. Spoon any remaining jam over fruit. Spread remaining one-third of pudding over fruit. Cover with plastic wrap. Chill for at least 2 hours. Garnish with peach slices and almonds.

◄ Sundae Dessert Bars

Patricia E. Hall
Geneva, Nebraska

Crust:
- 1 cup all-purpose flour
- ¼ cup packed brown sugar
- ¼ cup finely chopped nuts
- ½ cup butter or margarine, cut into ½-inch cubes

- 1 quart vanilla ice cream
- ½ cup chocolate fudge topping
- 1 cup dry roasted peanuts
- 2 cups prepared whipped topping

9 servings

In medium mixing bowl, combine flour, brown sugar and nuts. Cut in butter at low speed of electric mixer to form coarse crumbs. Press mixture firmly against bottom of 9-inch square baking dish. Place dish on saucer in microwave oven. Microwave at 70% (Medium High) for 6 to 8 minutes, or until crust appears dry and firm, rotating dish once. Cool completely.

Remove cover from ice cream. Place container in microwave oven. Microwave at 50% (Medium) for 45 seconds to 1 minute, or until softened. Spread ice cream over crust. Freeze for 1 to 2 hours, or until firm.

Place fudge topping in 1-cup measure. Microwave at 50% (Medium) for 45 seconds to 1 minute, or until warm. Pour topping evenly over ice cream. Sprinkle with peanuts. Pipe or spread whipped topping over peanuts. Cover with foil. Freeze for at least 4 hours, or until firm. Let stand for 5 to 10 minutes before serving.

Arctic Mousse

Jean Niedercorn
Waukesha, Wisconsin

Crust:
- ⅓ cup butter or margarine
- 1¼ cups graham cracker crumbs
- ¼ cup sugar

Filling:
- 2 squares (1 oz. each) unsweetened chocolate

- 1 jar (7 oz.) marshmallow creme
- 1 teaspoon vanilla
- 2 tablespoons milk
- 1 cup whipping cream, whipped

9 servings

Place butter in 9-inch square baking dish. Microwave at High for 1½ to 1¾ minutes, or until butter melts. Stir in graham cracker crumbs and sugar. Mix well. Press mixture firmly against bottom of dish. Microwave at High for 2 minutes, rotating dish once. Set aside.

Place chocolate in medium mixing bowl. Microwave at 50% (Medium) for 3 to 5 minutes, or until chocolate melts and can be stirred smooth, stirring once. Stir in marshmallow creme and vanilla. Blend in milk. Fold in whipped cream. Spread filling over prepared crust. Freeze for at least 4 hours. Cut into squares. Serve frozen.

Grandma White's Soft Serve ▲

A chocolate dessert similar to frozen pudding.

Loretta J. White
Sorrento, Florida

2 cups sugar	6 cups milk
½ cup all-purpose flour	4 cups half-and-half
2 tablespoons cocoa	1 teaspoon vanilla
5 eggs, slightly beaten	

½ gallon

In 5-quart casserole, combine sugar, flour and cocoa. Stir in eggs. Blend in milk and half-and-half using whisk. Microwave at High for 5 minutes. Beat with whisk. Reduce power to 70% (Medium High). Microwave for 30 minutes, stirring with whisk after every 10 minutes. Microwave at 70% (Medium High) for 9 to 13 minutes, or until mixture thickens and coats a metal spoon, beating with whisk after every 4 minutes. Blend in vanilla. Place casserole into 2 inches of cold water to stop cooking. Place sheet of plastic wrap directly on surface of custard. Cool slightly. Chill overnight. Freeze custard in ice cream freezer according to manufacturer's directions. Serve immediately, or store in freezer. If frozen solid, let stand at room temperature a few minutes to soften slightly before serving.

Creamy Chocolate Sauce ▲

Deborah D. Lathum
Highland, Indiana

½ cup light corn syrup
1 pkg. (6 oz.) semisweet chocolate chips
2 tablespoons butter or margarine
¼ cup half-and-half
½ teaspoon vanilla

About 1½ cups

Place corn syrup in 2-cup measure. Stir in chocolate chips and butter. Microwave at High for 1½ to 2 minutes, or until mixture can be stirred smooth, stirring after 1 minute. Blend in half-and-half and vanilla. Serve warm or cool over ice cream, cake or cream puffs.

Strawberry-Rhubarb Crisp

Barbara F. Aslakson
St. Louis Park, Minnesota

Topping:
1 cup quick-cooking rolled
   oats
½ cup all-purpose flour
½ cup packed brown sugar
⅓ cup granulated sugar
1 teaspoon ground cinnamon
½ teaspoon ground nutmeg
6 tablespoons butter or
   margarine, cut into ½-inch
   cubes

4 cups cut-up fresh rhubarb,
   ¾-inch pieces
3 tablespoons all-purpose flour
2 pkgs. (10 oz. each) frozen
   strawberries in syrup,
   thawed

6 to 8 servings

In medium mixing bowl, combine rolled oats, ½ cup flour, brown and granulated sugars, cinnamon and nutmeg. Mix well. Cut in butter to form fine crumbs. Set aside.

Place rhubarb in 2-quart casserole. Sprinkle with 3 tablespoons flour. Stir to coat. Cover. Microwave at High for 7 to 10 minutes, or until rhubarb is tender, stirring once. Stir in strawberries. Sprinkle topping evenly over rhubarb mixture. Reduce power to 70% (Medium High). Microwave, uncovered, for 10 to 13 minutes, or until bubbly in center, rotating casserole once. Serve warm with ice cream, if desired.

Blackberry Cobbler

Helen May
Salem, Oregon

¾ cup sugar
2 tablespoons cornstarch
½ teaspoon ground cinnamon
1 bag (16 oz.) frozen
   blackberries
1 teaspoon lemon juice

Topping:
1 tablespoon graham cracker
   crumbs
⅛ teaspoon ground nutmeg
¼ cup butter or margarine
2 cups buttermilk baking mix
1 tablespoon sugar
⅔ cup milk

6 servings

In 2-quart casserole, combine ¾ cup sugar, cornstarch and cinnamon. Stir in frozen blackberries and lemon juice. Microwave at High for 8 to 12 minutes, or until mixture is thickened and translucent, stirring twice. Set aside.

In custard cup, combine graham cracker crumbs and nutmeg. Set aside. Place butter in small mixing bowl. Microwave at High for 1¼ to 1½ minutes, or until butter melts. Add baking mix, sugar and milk. Stir until soft dough forms. Spoon six equal portions of dough onto hot blackberry mixture. Sprinkle tops of biscuits with graham cracker mixture. Microwave at High for 4 to 6 minutes, or until biscuits appear dry and are cooked through, rotating casserole once. Serve warm with cream.

Pumpkin Custard ▲

Cynthia J. Overby
Edwardsville, Illinois

Similar to pumpkin pie without the calories of the crust.

- 1 can (16 oz.) pumpkin
- 2 eggs, beaten
- 1 cup evaporated skimmed milk
- ⅓ cup packed brown sugar
- ¼ cup granulated sugar
- 1½ teaspoons ground cinnamon
- ½ teaspoon salt
- ¼ teaspoon ground ginger
- ¼ teaspoon ground nutmeg
  Whipped topping (optional)

6 servings

In medium mixing bowl, combine all ingredients, except whipped topping. Blend with whisk. Divide evenly among six 6-oz. custard cups. Arrange in circular pattern in microwave oven. Microwave at 50% (Medium) for 18 to 23 minutes, or until centers are soft-set, rearranging and rotating cups 2 or 3 times. Serve warm or cool. Garnish with dollop of whipped topping.

Apple Bread Pudding ▲

Margaret Kaatz
Kansas City, Missouri

- 3 eggs
- ⅔ cup packed brown sugar
- 1 teaspoon ground cinnamon
- ¼ teaspoon salt
- ¼ teaspoon ground nutmeg
- 1 teaspoon vanilla
- 2 cups milk
- 4 cups chopped apples
- 3 cups unseasoned whole wheat and white croutons
- ½ cup raisins

Sauce:

- ½ cup packed brown sugar
- ¼ cup butter or margarine
- ¼ cup amaretto liqueur

6 to 8 servings

In large mixing bowl, blend eggs, brown sugar, cinnamon, salt, nutmeg and vanilla. Blend in milk. Stir in apples, croutons and raisins. Mix well. Pour into 2-quart casserole.

Place casserole on saucer in microwave oven. Microwave at High for 5 minutes. Stir. Reduce power to 70% (Medium High). Microwave for 14 to 17 minutes, or until apples are tender and mixture appears set, stirring twice. Set aside.

In small mixing bowl, combine all sauce ingredients. Microwave at High for 2 to 3 minutes, or until bubbly, stirring once. Serve over warm pudding.

Old-Fashioned ▲ Rice Pudding

Penny Dunbar
Green Bay, Wisconsin

- 1 can (12 oz.) evaporated milk
- ¼ cup milk
- 1 tablespoon butter or margarine
- ⅓ cup sugar
- ⅓ cup raisins
- 2 eggs, beaten
- ¼ teaspoon salt
- 1 teaspoon vanilla
- 4 cups cooked rice
  Ground nutmeg (optional)

6 to 8 servings

In 4-cup measure, combine evaporated milk, milk and butter. Microwave at High for 2½ minutes. In 2-quart casserole, combine sugar, raisins, eggs, salt and vanilla. Mix well. Blend hot milk mixture slowly into egg mixture. Stir in rice. Microwave at High for 3 minutes. Stir. Reduce power to 50% (Medium). Microwave for 8 to 15 minutes, or until mixture thickens, stirring 2 or 3 times. Sprinkle with nutmeg. Serve warm.

Glorified Rice Pudding

Mrs. Elaine Spessard
Greers Ferry, Arkansas

6 tablespoons sugar, divided
4 teaspoons cornstarch
⅛ teaspoon salt
½ cup milk
1 can (8 oz.) crushed
    pineapple in juice, drained
    (reserve juice)
2 eggs, separated
½ teaspoon vanilla
⅛ teaspoon cream of tartar
1½ cups cooked rice
¼ cup maraschino cherries,
    cut up, drained

6 to 8 servings

In medium mixing bowl, combine ¼ cup sugar, cornstarch and salt. Blend in milk. Stir in pineapple juice. Reserve pineapple. Microwave at High for 4 to 6 minutes, or until mixture is thickened and translucent, stirring 3 times. In custard cup, beat egg yolks. Blend small amount of hot mixture into egg yolks. Add back to hot mixture, stirring constantly. Reduce power to 50% (Medium). Microwave for 45 seconds to 1 minute, or until mixture thickens. Stir in vanilla. Set aside.

In medium mixing bowl, combine egg whites and cream of tartar. Beat until foamy. Gradually add remaining 2 tablespoons sugar, beating until stiff peaks form. Fold egg whites into hot pudding. Fold in pineapple, rice and maraschino cherries. Cover. Chill for at least 4 hours. Serve with whipped cream, if desired.

Marshmallows ▲

Mrs. Janet Ellsworth
Corning, New York

Vegetable cooking spray
6 tablespoons powdered
    sugar, divided
3 envelopes (.25 oz. each)
    unflavored gelatin
12 tablespoons water, divided

2 cups granulated sugar
⅛ teaspoon salt
1 teaspoon vanilla or ½
    teaspoon orange extract

About 1 lb.

Spray 9-inch square baking dish with vegetable cooking spray. Sift 2 tablespoons powdered sugar evenly over bottom of dish. Set aside. Place gelatin in small mixing bowl. Pour 6 tablespoons water over gelatin. Let stand to soften. Meanwhile, in 2-quart measure, combine granulated sugar, remaining 6 tablespoons water and salt. Microwave at High for 2 minutes. Mix well. Insert microwave candy thermometer. Microwave at High for 3 to 4½ minutes, or until thermometer registers 234°F (soft ball stage). Syrup forms a soft ball which flattens when removed from cold water. Add softened gelatin and vanilla. Beat at low speed of electric mixer until blended. Beat at high speed until mixture is very thick, about 8 to 10 minutes. Spread into prepared dish. Sift 1 tablespoon powdered sugar evenly over top. Chill for at least 4 hours, or until set.

Sift 1 tablespoon powdered sugar onto board. Loosen edges and lift marshmallow mixture onto prepared board. Sift remaining 2 tablespoons powdered sugar into small bowl. Cut marshmallows into small squares using kitchen shears or knife dipped in boiling water. Roll all sides of each marshmallow in powdered sugar. Place marshmallows on wire rack. Cover with paper towel and allow to dry, about 3 hours. Store in covered container between sheets of wax paper.

Chocolate Pizza

Sharon Allen
Wichita, Kansas

Candy can be spread into a heart shape or into smaller circles.

1½ cups semisweet chocolate chips
1 cup butterscotch chips
¾ cup miniature marshmallows
¾ cup chopped dry roasted peanuts
¾ cup crushed ripple potato chips
2 tablespoons flaked coconut
13 maraschino cherries, cut in half and drained (optional)
¼ cup candy coated plain chocolate pieces
4 oz. white candy coating, broken into squares
1 teaspoon vegetable shortening

1¾ lbs. candy

Draw 10-inch circle on parchment paper. Place on baking sheet. Set aside. In medium mixing bowl, combine chocolate and butterscotch chips. Microwave at 50% (Medium) for 4 to 6 minutes, or until chocolate melts and can be stirred smooth, stirring once. Stir in marshmallows, peanuts and potato chips. Mix well to coat. Spread mixture evenly to cover 10-inch circle. Sprinkle with coconut. Top pizza with maraschino cherries and chocolate pieces. Set aside.

In 2-cup measure, combine candy coating and shortening. Microwave at 50% (Medium) for 3 to 4 minutes, or until candy coating melts and can be stirred smooth, stirring once. Drizzle over chocolate pizza. Chill for at least 1½ hours, or until set. Peel off parchment paper. Place on serving plate.

Best-Ever Fudge ▲

Jan Testa
New Castle, Pennsylvania

1 pkg. (6 oz.) semisweet chocolate chips
6 oz. baking sweet chocolate, broken into squares
1 cup chopped nuts
1 cup marshmallow creme
2¼ cups sugar
1 can (5 oz.) evaporated milk
1 tablespoon butter or margarine
⅛ teaspoon salt

2½ lbs. candy

Butter 9-inch square baking dish. Set aside. In large mixing bowl, combine chocolate chips, sweet chocolate, nuts and marshmallow creme. Set aside.

In 2-quart measure, combine sugar, evaporated milk, butter and salt. Mix well. Microwave at High for 2 minutes, stirring after every minute. Microwave at High for 1½ to 4 minutes, or until mixture comes to a full rolling boil. Pour hot milk mixture over chocolate mixture. Mix until chocolate melts and marshmallow creme is blended. Spread mixture evenly into prepared dish. Chill until cool and set, about 3 hours. Cut into small squares.

Rich Layered Bars ▲

Karma J. Virgil
Grand Junction, Colorado

6 tablespoons butter or margarine
1½ cups graham cracker crumbs
3 tablespoons sugar
2 cups flaked coconut
1 pkg. (6 oz.) semisweet chocolate chips
1 pkg. (6 oz.) butterscotch chips
1 cup chopped pecans
1 can (14 oz.) sweetened condensed milk (not evaporated)

3 dozen bars

Place butter in 9-inch square baking dish. Microwave at High for 1½ to 1¾ minutes, or until butter melts. Stir in graham cracker crumbs and sugar. Mix well. Press mixture firmly against bottom of dish. Microwave at High for 2 minutes, rotating dish once. Layer coconut, chocolate chips, butterscotch chips and pecans over crust. Pour sweetened condensed milk evenly over pecans. Reduce power to 50% (Medium). Microwave for 10 to 18 minutes, or just until bubbly around edges. Cool completely. Cut into squares.

Caramel Nut Candy ▲

Shirley Kernen
Del Norte, Colorado

1½ cups sugar
⅓ cup milk
¼ cup butter or margarine
1 bag (14 oz.) caramels, unwrapped
¾ cup chopped nuts

2 lbs. candy

Butter 9-inch square baking dish. Set aside. In 2-quart measure, combine sugar, milk and butter. Microwave at High for 2 minutes. Stir until butter melts. Insert microwave candy thermometer. Microwave at High for 3 to 4½ minutes, or until thermometer registers 234°F (soft ball stage). Syrup forms a soft ball which flattens when removed from cold water. Remove thermometer. Carefully add caramels. Microwave at High for 1½ to 2½ minutes, or until caramels melt and can be stirred smooth. Stir in nuts. Spread mixture evenly into prepared dish. Chill until cool and set, about 3 hours. Cut into small squares.

Recipe Contributors

153

Index

157